COME FISHING WITH ME

Come Fishing With Me

PETER STONE

PELHAM BOOKS

First published in Great Britain by Pelham Books Ltd
52 Bedford Square, London, W.C.1
1973

© 1973 by Peter Stone

All Rights Reserved. No part of this publication may be recorded, stored in a retrieval system, or transmitted, in any form or by any means, electronic, mechanical, photocopying, recording or otherwise, without the prior permission of the Copyright owner

7207 0663 7

Set and printed in Great Britain by Tonbridge Printers Ltd, Peach Hall Works, Tonbridge, Kent, in Plantin ten on twelve point on paper supplied by P. F. Bingham Ltd, and bound by James Burn at Esher, Surrey

CONTENTS

Introduction p. 11
1 Thames barbel p. 13
2 The Kennet at Theale p. 22
3 Snowberry Lake p. 30
4 The swing to the sea p. 34
5 Blenheim Lake p. 42
6 The Upper Ouse p. 49
7 Opportunism: my first five-pound chub p. 58
8 Days amongst the bream p. 64
9 Trout on the fly p. 74
10 Creek mullet p. 79
11 Fishing for television p. 81
12 Tench p. 87
13 Annan chub p. 95
14 Royalty barbel p. 100
15 1963 Freeze-up p. 105
16 A gravel pit p. 110
17 Roach and dace on Opera p. 123
Index p. 127

ILLUSTRATIONS

Between pages 64 and 65

Ted Robbins weighs his big barbel

A 'cat' . . . not a pleasant sight

Bringing a 30 lb. tope to the side

The author and tope

Returning a nice Blenheim pike

A 17 lb. pike finally beaten

Fred Towns and Blenheim pike

A 5 lb. 2 oz. Thames chub

A 27 lb. catch of Thames chub

130 lb. of bream

A Test trout taken on a fly

Gravel-pit tench

Annan chub

Walking along the frozen Thames

A roach that weighed $2\frac{1}{4}$ lb.

ACKNOWLEDGEMENTS

My thanks are due to the Editors of *Shooting Times, Angling, Anglers' Mail* and *Angling Telegraph* for permission to use articles already published. To Fred J. Taylor, who not only read my manuscript but who has also helped me in many ways; to Tony Fordham, rod maker of Poole, for listening to my suggestions and producing rods to my specifications; to Ron Cook for reading the proofs; to Janet Bowman for typing the manuscript; and to Richard Walker who encouraged me in my writing almost fifteen years ago.

To my companions Fred Towns, John Everard and Ted Robbins, with whom I have spent many happy hours, and to others too numerous to mention, without whose help this book would never have been written. To ace float maker Peter Drennan, for making sure that I am never short of floats – which, on countless occasions have played their part in the capture of big fish.

Lastly, but by no means least, to my wife Sue, for not only accepting my sport but also for making my friends so welcome. To her I am truly grateful.

Introduction

In 1961 my good friend Fred J. Taylor wrote *Favourite Swims*. That book, one of the most enjoyable it has been my pleasure to read, inspired me and I vowed that, one day, I too would write such a book. Not that I could ever hope to emulate Fred, but I thought I had something to tell. This book is the result.

It is not a 'how to catch them' book, but an account of some of my best – and not so best – days spent in pursuit of many different species both freshwater and sea. But it is not entirely a book of reminiscences; I have tried – and I hope succeeded – to tell how fish can be caught, and of the methods I use to achieve that end. I am not suggesting that my methods are the best – far from it – but, used in the right place at the right time, they work. They catch big fish, too.

The chapter on sea fishing may surprise some who think of me as a freshwater angler pure and simple. But I am not: I have spent many happy hours afloat at sea and have caught some good fish in the process. Ever since that day when, in company with that grand old angler Bill Warren, I caught my first tope, I have been a confirmed sea angler. Conger, skate and shark excepted, there is, in my opinion, no finer sport than catching sea fish on freshwater gear, for weight-for-weight sea fish fight better than their freshwater counterparts – always providing that one is using the right tackle, of course.

And there is fly fishing – another great sport which I enjoy so much. I remember in my 'teens catching big chub on Zulus and other big busy flies from under overhanging trees along the Thames, and on the shallows at the 'tail' of weirpools numbers of dace on flies, the names of which I can't remember. From chub I graduated to trout, firstly on the delightful, meandering river Windrush, from which I have taken vast numbers on both wet and dry fly (I'm no purist!), to the wonderful Test in Hampshire, where, whilst I was writing this book, Fred Taylor gave me a day and where I caught my biggest trout to date, a rainbow of 4 lb. 10 oz. This fish, which I had to stalk by crawling on my stomach and which entailed putting my fly accurately amongst dense weedbeds, gave me an enormous amount of pleasure. One day I hope to catch a really big trout on a fly.

In chapter one I write about barbel, and how my friends and I catch them at night in winter – Brr! This, I believe, is something new in barbel fishing (although there is a lot of truth in the saying there is nothing new in fishing), for until recently barbel, like carp, were considered to be 'summer fish' only, which went into a state of semi-hibernation and only fed in times of high water. Today we know different, and one day I will write a book about 'off-beat' barbel techniques.

Although I, like most anglers, enjoy catching big fish, I have not lost my sense of values, and I still get an enormous kick when I catch a medium-sized fish in either exceptional circumstances or difficult conditions. Fred Taylor says that fishing should be fun – and he's right. My fishing, like Fred's, isn't a chore; I enjoy my sport and God's glorious open air and all that goes with it.

So... come fishing with me!

1. *Thames barbel*

My baptism to specimen hunting started when I was about ten. Close to my home a bridge spans the Thames, below which is a pool some forty yards long with an average depth of six feet. At the 'tail' the water shallows rapidly, and in normal summer conditions it is possible to walk across in gumboots. The pool has three lashers, which in those days held fish of most species, including some very large trout which I hopefully, but unsuccessfully, fished for during the months of May and June. But it wasn't only trout which fed on those shallows; barbel, large shoals of them, would appear during May and early June, feeding ravenously on the vast shoals of minnows which inhabited the river.

Imagine it: shoals of barbel with their dorsal fins above the surface chasing minnows, and I, a mere boy, standing on the bridge with a can of 'red soldiers' at the ready. (How pretty a spawning minnow is with its red and green flanks; we called them 'red soldiers' – and I can't think of a better name.) Those large dorsals fascinated me, and the close season meant little. So I fished for, and caught, barbel – many of them big ones. And the manner in which I caught them was exciting fishing indeed.

My rod was tonkin cane (which I still have and nowadays, money can't buy), the reel, a centre-pin on which I had 100 yards of plaited silk line. The trace was 'Jagut', the hook, a No. 8 tied to gut. My float was a small cork, cut in half with a stick to hold it in position. Twelve inches from the hook was a small drilled bullet. Crude? Maybe – but it caught fish. The minnow was hooked through the top lip only.

Standing on the bridge I can remember trotting the minnow down the centre lasher until it reached the 'tail'. As the minnow trundled along the bottom a big dorsal would turn towards it, followed, seconds later, by the cork disappearing rapidly. A long, sweeping strike and the hook was set with the barbel coming upstream towards me. Now came the tricky part. Holding the rod up high I walked along the road (not much traffic in those days) towards the side of the bridge, ducked under the railings, transferred the rod from one hand to the other, then went down the bank to the edge of the pool where the battle was fought out. Night after night I did this 'performing act', and caught countless numbers of barbel up to 8 lb. and over. Sometimes I caught a nice trout; most nights good chub – and always barbel.

Below the shallows was another swim. Here thick patches of ranunculus covered the river and barbel could be seen 'flashing' beneath the weed. Here, too, a trotted minnow proved deadly, with the barbel, on average, bigger. In this swim I took many over seven pounds, a few 'eights' and one 'nine'. I always used a float – I never thought to leger!

Further down river was another swim, a narrow channel between dense patches of lilies. It was in this swim that I discovered that barbel were not primarily bottom feeders, for on sunny days they could be seen basking a foot or so below the surface, and occasionally twisting over taking in food. So I fished a minnow just below the surface – and caught barbel. Here they were much bigger – seven to eight pounds on average. By the time I was sixteen I was a confirmed barbel addict, and have remained so to this day.

In the autumn of 1964 I received information that some large barbel were being caught from the Thames right in the middle of Oxford. I had never fished the reach before (to do so meant sitting on the pavement!), but one evening I decided to have a try. I arrived at dusk and twenty minutes later the rod top pulled over an inch; I struck, and after a good scrap landed one of 9 lb. The following night I copped a slightly smaller fish, and followed this up with other good barbel. Naturally the word got around, and one day an angler asked me to catch one for him. I love a challenge, so I took him along. I elected to use flake (don't ask me why – I had never used it there before) and within minutes of casting had a good bite which I missed. 'Never mind,' I said, 'I'll have him next time – just you see.' It was a long cast, but I dropped another piece of flake bang on target; the bait hit bottom, I took up the slack, and thought I saw the rod top move. And when I 'think' I strike! As I did so, the clutch screamed out and a minute later an eight-pounder came sliding over the net. At that the chap packed, picked up his bike, and, with a 'well done!', departed. For the remainder of the evening I didn't have another bite.

Several years later I took a course in salmon fly casting, which took place adjacent to my old barbel swim amongst the lilies. For various reasons I hadn't fished it for years, but knowing that my lessons would finish well before dark I took my gear along. Lessons over, I tackled up with one swan shot on a 6-lb. b.s. line and a lob with a No. 6 hook pushed through its head *once*. (You catch more barbel if you hook a lob this way.) Because of the lilies the swim isn't easy to fish, and after casting, the rod *must* be held high so the line doesn't touch the lilies running parallel with both banks. I cast the lob into the channel; it touched bottom and, to my surprise, the line tightened. Before I could say 'barbel' the fish was in the lilies *and taking line*. Leaping off my stool I took to the water and by 'pumping' (how easy it is to 'pump' a barbel out of weeds!) finally got him into the channel and into the net. Five minutes later I was into another, then, as darkness fell, all went quiet. These two barbel remain firmly embedded in my memory because I caught them after a lapse of many years in one of my boyhood swims.

Naturally I fished there again – the following night in fact! I usually caught one, sometimes two, all between six and seven pounds. Of course I couldn't keep the swim to myself, and was sometimes beaten to it (on one occasion at 3 a.m.!), but most anglers couldn't handle the barbel amongst the dense lilies; consequently, many were hooked and lost and they eventually became shy. Only once did I find them really 'on', when I caught four and lost one.

It came about like this. I had promised to fish a match, but heavy rain at mid-day dampened (pardon the pun!) my enthusiasm somewhat. Towards evening the rain eased a little and I decided to give the barbel a try. 'I'll come,' Sue said, and half an hour later we were both huddled under my umbrella. Terminal tackle was two swan shot on a sliding link stopped 12 inches from a size 6 hook. My supply of lobs was, unfortunately, exhausted, but I had plenty of brandlings – one of my favourite baits.

It was raining heavily and – not very hopefully – I made my first cast. Why, I don't know, but I have seldom done well in heavy rain and I had to make the best of it.

Several times during the next half hour the line trembled; sometimes I struck, sometimes I didn't. Then, suddenly, after two preliminary twitches, the line tightened. I struck, and a fish was on.

Now you have to know what to do in this swim, and I immediately leapt from my seat and walked into the water. Failure to do this, I had found, resulted in the fish turning towards you and entering the dense weedbeds. This was why so many anglers hooked and lost their fish – they didn't know the drill!

My 'Specimen' rod is $11\frac{1}{2}$ ft., which enabled me to push the rod top right out into the channel where I could apply maximum sidestrain. Two or three minutes later it was in the net – a five-pounder. This was encouraging, and I was soon waiting for the next bite. It didn't take long.

Once more, two twitches then the slow, confident pull, and again I found myself standing knee deep in water with the reel screaming. This one, too, was eventually netted, and proved to be the same size as the first.

The wind and rain had now ceased. Although it was nowhere near dark thick mist was rising, for the water temperature at 65° F. was much warmer than the air. Everything was quiet and a feeling of expectancy – something that cannot be described – hung in the air.

Several minutes later the line twitched once more, followed

by a good pull. Contact was made but soon lost, for immediately the fish turned, the line broke above the hook. I cursed my luck. I hate losing fish, especially when I don't know what I have done wrong. But time was valuable and another hook was quickly attached.

One enormous lob was keeping my brandlings company. 'Let's give one a treat,' I said, and placing the hook through the worm at the top of its head I cast alongside the lilies. Why, I don't know, but barbel appear to prefer a lob hooked in this manner. It has certainly paid off with me.

My tackle had hardly settled before I was into another fish. I knew immediately that this was a better one, for, before I could get off my stool, some ten yards of line had been stripped off the reel. I gave it all I had and to my delight, I turned it.

For several minutes I experienced one of the finest scraps any fish has given me; long, powerful runs interspersed with short rushes into the weeds. Sometimes I held him out, sometimes I didn't, but continual 'pumping' always brought him into the channel again. Finally he rolled over into my big net – 9 lb. exactly. Not a specimen perhaps, but a very big fish for the water.

I then sat down and had a breather. Mist was now rising heavily from the water and it was nearly dark. I sat and pondered; could I get an even bigger one whilst they were still going? Well, there was still time.

I turned to the wife. 'Do you know,' I said, 'one of the beauties of barbel fishing is that you never know just how big or small the next one is going to be. Unlike some species they do not shoal according to size; if you hook one it could be 4 lb. or 14 lb.'

There was time for just one more cast. Hastily I put four brandlings on the hook and cast right into the lilies. A few minutes elapsed, and I was just thinking of packing when the line trembled. Almost immediately the top pulled over, I struck, and the fish was on. This one, however, came straight towards me and, with one pull, landed right in my lap – 8 oz.!

Sue and I looked at each other and both burst out laughing. As I said, you never can tell.

In September 1969 I entered hospital for an operation and it was mid-October before I got fishing again. I was still convalescing, and one morning I decided to give the barbel a try where, five years earlier, I had caught the eight-pounder 'to order'.

In less than an hour I had four bites – two barbel, two chub. That year the ban on night fishing in the Thames had been lifted, so the Oxford Specimen Group immediately decided to give them a try at night.

To cut a long story short, the members (I was out of the act as the business of striking hurt me too much) caught several big barbel, the best being 10¾ lb. Some were taken at dusk, but most were caught well after darkness had fallen.

One night, Ted Robbins had been fishing a 'hot-spot' for two hours without a bite and decided to move to a swim fifty yards upstream. The time was half past nine. He cast, put his rod down to light his pipe and as he did so his rod, to quote Ted, 'was swept along the bank'. He managed to grab the handle before it disappeared completely, and eventually landed a barbel weighing 10½ lb.

That fish set me thinking. Did barbel wander at night? Would it be advisable to keep moving until contact was made? Would fishing right through the night (even in winter) produce even more barbel, for, remember, these fish were being taken very late? All this was under consideration when the first frost came and – against our better judgement I think – we decided to give them best.

But one member, Bob Hastings (like Fred Towns with the roach, as you will read later), was made of sterner stuff. In February a bitterly cold east wind blew up and stayed with us for several days. Then, on the Saturday evening, the phone rang. It was Bob.

'Going to catch a barbel tomorrow morning,' he said, 'starting at 5 a.m. – coming?'

'You're going to do *what?*' I replied.

THAMES BARBEL

'Catch a barbel' said Bob,' – see you there!'

I told him what I thought of the idea, filled a hot-water bottle, and went to bed.

Next morning I went pike fishing and was huddled under my brolly when Sue appeared. 'Bob has just phoned,' she said, 'he's got two barbel – could you go and photograph them?'

I arrived to find Bob playing yet another good fish, which he unfortunately lost. I asked him when he had caught his two fish (the best $8\frac{1}{2}$ lb.). 'At 5 a.m.' he said. 'Had one first cast, the other soon after.'

Now I had caught barbel in winter before but never by design, so this raised a question. Did barbel (as was generally believed) go into a state of hibernation in winter, or didn't they? The more I thought about it the more interesting it sounded. I decided to try them at night, in winter.

John Everard was the first member to try in 1970. It was December and the river was fining down after a flood. John arrived at dusk and lost a barbel first cast. On the next cast he copped one of $8\frac{1}{4}$ lb., then lost another.

I joined him the next night. I missed a perfectly good bite first cast – then nothing. I went home wondering whether, after all, it was worth the effort for, believe me, dragging oneself away from a roaring fire in December *does* require some effort.

But I need not have worried. From then on we fished regularly for barbel at night and, although we didn't exactly set the world alight, we caught, and lost, enough to convince us that one was always in with a chance – and a good one.

One day I was stopped by a chap who asked how I had been faring lately. The previous night I had caught two nice barbel, and I told him so. 'I would love to catch a barbel,' he said, 'never caught one.' 'Well,' I replied, 'it's not difficult but... you *must* drag yourself away from the fireside.'

That night John and I fished the swim of the previous evening. It was bitterly cold with a gale-force east wind blowing downstream. At 9 p.m. we packed – our fingers were numbed – and when I arrived home this chap was waiting for me. 'What a night,' he said (I nodded in agreement!), 'caught two, best eight pounds – and lost four more. Caught one first cast – bait had hardly touched bottom and the others all followed within an hour.' What a night indeed!

This brings me to the all-important question of confidence. I can't divulge locations for obvious reasons, but this particular reach where my friends fished had, for several years, regularly produced double-figure barbel. But not for me: in fact I have yet to catch just one barbel from there! One evening several years ago I was broke twice in two casts but, apart from that, I don't think I have ever had a bite from one. It's the only reach of water in the country I have fished regularly for barbel and never caught one.*

My friend had never fished there before but, thinking it was where I had caught mine the previous evening, went there full of confidence. When I first met Bob Hastings, he, too, badly wanted a barbel, and that was the reach he chose for his 'christening' and where, incidentally, he caught those two at 5 a.m. one February morning. I know several other chaps who, thinking I catch barbel there, have gone and clobbered one. As I say, it's all a question of confidence – the reason perhaps why I have failed: I haven't much left!

During the closing weeks of the '70–'71 season our Group decided to concentrate on this reach. One night John Everard caught a 'seven' – first cast! – and several others were taken by other anglers, including one of 11¼ lb. And that brings me to another point. Another friend, Paul, decided to 'hammer' one swim on this reach and set aside one complete week in March for it. There were two evenings he couldn't go; the Tuesday and Friday.

On the Tuesday I fished the swim. I had two bites and caught two chub, best 4½ lb. On the Friday another angler fished there and copped a barbel, 11¼ lb. And Paul? Not a smell all week!

* This was written during the winter of 1970. In June 1971, on my first visit of the season and on the second cast, I broke my 'duck' and followed this up with another several nights later. My convictions stated in the last paragraph are now even stronger!

THAMES BARBEL

It appears to me therefore that to be successful one *must* go night after night, bashing away until successful: miss a night, and that night might be *the* one. There is no telling when they will feed, for as yet we have very few pointers to go on. Certainly flood water brings them on (I always knew that anyway) but we caught them in all weathers, gales, east winds, frosts – the lot.

Bearing in mind the number of barbel caught 'first cast', I firmly believe it pays to keep moving swims. As a rule I give a swim an hour before I move, but I can't help wondering whether even this is too long. By the time this appears in print I hope to know a little more, because I consider it a highly important question if one wishes to be consistently successful with winter barbel at night.

For years I longed for the day when I could fish the Thames at night, for I always maintained that big barbel fed more freely at that time. But I must be honest, never, in my wildest dreams, did I imagine they did so in winter – especially when it was bitterly cold. But, despite the short time we have been fishing for them, I think we have proved that night fishing in winter gives one a very fair chance of success. No doubt there is much we don't know – and never will – but I expect to add to my knowledge as each winter passes, thereby increasing my chances.*

What I can't understand, however, is my total lack of success in that one particular reach mentioned earlier, for I have fished it long and very hard indeed. Perhaps I fish too hard – I don't know – but of one thing I am sure; one day I shall land a really tremendous barbel from there. Don't ask me why; I just don't know. But I can feel it in my bones!

---

* Since writing the above another winter has passed, a winter which proved beyond any doubt that not only can barbel be caught at night, but that many nights are more favourable than those in summer and autumn.

2. The Kennet at Theale

Several years ago Dick Walker, the Taylors, a few others, and I rented a reach of the Kennet. The first time I saw the water I fell in love with it, for it was one of the most compact fisheries I have seen. Running parallel with the river was a canal, and in between there was a little lake. This was joined to both waters by a sluice gate, of which you will read later.

The Kennet held a vast head of barbel and although their average size (three to four pounds) was nothing to shout about, their numbers compensated, insomuch that we could always catch some. The river contained a lot of ranunculus, so one could fish quite fine and get away with it. For, in my experience, providing you get downstream of the fish, landing barbel in ranunculus is kid's stuff, and these Kennet barbel were no exception.

At that time, Dick Walker and Billy Lane had never met, so one morning I took Billy, his son Alan, and two others over to meet Dick. To say the day was hilarious is putting it mildly. Both Billy and Alan badly wanted a barbel so I took Alan 'under my wing'. Fred put Billy in the best swim in the fishery and I wandered off upstream with Alan to another 'hot-spot'.

To fish the swim meant poking the rod over an overhanging hawthorn and dropping the bait in the water under it. Rarely did the swim let me down, and a bite invariably occurred within thirty seconds of the bait touching bottom. I warned Alan of this, and told him to be ready.

He wiggled his bait first over, then under the bush (I don't think Alan went much on it), and I watched his line drop slack as the bait settled. As it did so, the rod top pulled over two feet – and Alan didn't move! 'Blimey, that was quick,' he said as the rod straightened out, 'you were right'. He didn't get another chance.

We rejoined Dick and Billy at tea-time. Bill hadn't caught a barbel; Dick hadn't even started fishing! Bill had been pumping in maggots all day and against Dick's advice had taken off the leger in favour of a float. Blimey, how Bill murdered those roach and dace – every throw a winner – but no barbel. And it was barbel he wanted.

It was almost dusk when Dick Walker spoke. 'Well,' he said, 'if Lane can't catch one I suppose I had better show him how.' He fetched his tackle. Bill, as I have said, had been pumping in maggots all day, a fact which hadn't gone unnoticed by Dick. On a No. 8 hook Dick threaded a huge bunch of maggots and cast at the 'tail' of Bill's swim. Within ten seconds he was into one and asked Bill to bring the net. Stooping down, Bill produced his, and with net in hand crouched down alongside Dick. Dick took one look at Billy's not over-large net and exclaimed 'I asked for a landing net, not a bloody tea-strainer!' By this time I was ready with mine, and I shall never forget the look on Bill's face as Dick removed the hook. 'Can't think what you've been mucking about at all day,' Dick remarked, 'nothing to it.'

But that was not all. As Dick slid the barbel back, Joe, whom we hadn't seen all day, arrived on the scene. 'Um,' said Joe, looking at the river immediately below Bill, 'think I'll catch myself a nice chub.' At this point the river was dense with ranunculus, with a very small channel running along the opposite bank. Placing a large piece of cheese on his hook, Joe, with not a little accuracy, placed his bait in the channel, lifted the rod to keep the line clear of the weed – then struck. As he did so, he gave one almighty overhead pull and a three-pound chub came protesting to the surface. Joe quickly pointed the rod at the water, wound, and the chub came sliding over the weed like a bleak, straight into his net. It was all over in 30 seconds! 'Bah gum,' said Bill's mate, 'never seen bluudy fish come over water like that before – never.' I still laugh about it now.

Later that night we all climbed back into Bill's van and waved Fred and Dick goodbye. As Bill drove off we were almost deafened by the banging on the side coming from outside. 'A reet rare lad that Walker,' Bill said, 'a reet rare lad.'

During the seven years we fished Theale we caught barbel as we pleased. We didn't catch any big ones – my personal best was two fish a little over six pounds – good fish for the water. It rarely let us down, although it nearly did once. I had been asked to catch one for a film and the only date I had free was in late November. It was a bitterly cold day; worse still, it rained. I fished hard, and the only bite came during late afternoon just when the cameraman was deciding whether he had enough light left or not. Luckily I hooked and landed the fish, which, on a 3-lb. b.s. line in fast water, showed up well in the film.

We caught barbel from most points along the river but, strangely enough, the most barbelly-looking swim never produced anything. This particular swim ran under the far bank and could only be reached from an island in the middle of the river. And you could only wade out to it when the river was low. I fished the swim at every opportunity as did several others, but it was always 'dead'. Until one morning, that is.

Dick Walker and Pete Thomas had arrived the evening before and we all rose at dawn for an onslaught on the barbel. We were not very hopeful, however, because dawn never proved productive; indeed, you were lucky to get even a bite. Midday, evening and night were the best times – never dawn.

I decided to fish the 'island' swim and had been given a new reel for testing. The previous evening I had caught a crayfish and decided to give it a try. I waded out to the island, placed a No. 2 hook in the crayfish's tail and cast against the far bank.

Five minutes later I thought I saw the line move but wasn't sure – so I struck. A heavy fish turned slowly downstream and made off along the bank. I was fishing fairly heavy – 8-lb. b.s. line and a Mark IV – and piled on the pressure. Now I have always said (not boastfully) that once I hook a fish he's mine – providing nothing unforeseen happens. But the unforeseen *did* happen – and how! I was gently pumping the fish towards me – and it *was* a good fish – when the reel handle suddenly collapsed; the line fell slack, and he was gone.

But for me the main interest of the fishery didn't lie in the river but the little lake. We knew it held tench, so naturally we fished for them. But could we catch them – could we heck! We tried just about everything and at every possible hour but it was no good; the tench just didn't want to know.

During the following close season Ken Morritt decided – against Fred's advice – to stock it with trout, and during the next few weeks we enjoyed good fun with the fly rod. June came and Joe Taylor and I decided to fish it on opening day for tench. Dawn broke; and at 5 a.m. we packed – we couldn't stop catching trout! Even enormous pieces of crust failed to deter them, and after unhooking thirty-five I gave them best.

Two weeks later I fished the lake again. I didn't catch a tench – but I didn't catch a trout either. Neither did anyone else that weekend, nor the next, nor the next...

In November that year the Taylors, Pete Drennan and I decided to see whether the lake held any pike, and we turned up one morning with a can of live-bait. I won't go into details, but our two-day total amounted to 54, up to $11\frac{1}{2}$ lb., all of which we tipped into the river. That weekend we learnt two things: firstly, the lake held pike; secondly, we knew where the trout had gone!

The lake also held big roach, and not long after we spent a day after them – or at least part of the day. It was very, very cold and as nothing was doing Fred suggested we should 'stir 'em up a bit'. I have already mentioned the two sluice gates at either end of the lake, so Fred and I lifted the one joining the lake to the canal. The water gushed in through a narrow channel then over some mud flats. As it did so the water gradually thickened until it was the colour of pea soup. We hadn't reckoned on this but, it was now too late. We also hadn't reckoned on the events which were to follow.

As we reached our swim – now 'boiling' somewhat – I saw a tench roll – then another. Now, like most anglers, I have caught tench in rivers in winter in times of flood and wasn't it flood conditions we had created? Of course! We had activated the tench into feeding.

Details don't matter but we caught several good tench that morning, and on all other days in winter when we opened the sluice gates. Not once, in six years of fishing, did I fail to catch a tench in winter.

As I have said, we had a compact little fishery, and we decided to make ourselves comfortable. Nearby was an old disused pill-box; this, we thought, would make an ideal weekend retreat. And so it proved; we slept, ate and dined in comfort. And we had fun.

We fished Theale most weekends, arriving on the Friday evening and returning home on the Sunday. The pill-box provided cover and sleeping accommodation and, as I have said, we could eat in comfort. But sleep, that was different; most nights it was bedlam inside that 'box'.

One night Fred 'did his nut'. We had just settled down, having planned a dawn onslaught on the barbel. But Fred couldn't sleep and, to quote Fred: 'When Fred can't sleep nobody else does either.' He eventually decided to sleep nude and, getting out of bed, peeled off, stood up, patted himself from head to foot and exclaimed 'That's better, never again shall I sleep in pyjamas.' Peter Drennan was there and I thought he would never stop laughing.

Finally Fred got into bed. It was my job to rouse the others so I set my alarm clock, which had a rather loud tick.

'Turn that bloody thing off Stoney,' said Fred, 'I can't sleep. Go on, turn it off.'

I said nothing, pretending to be asleep. Suddenly there was a terrific din enough to waken the dead as my alarm was sent hurtling along the floor, coming to rest against the far wall. Fred had thrown his slipper at it.

'That's better,' said Fred, 'perhaps I can now get some sleep.'

In less than a minute he was away – snoring. Remember? 'If Fred can't sleep nobody else does either.' Very true. Trouble is, you don't get to sleep when he's asleep either. My, how Fred snores!

On another occasion he couldn't get off because Mother Nature was calling but he was too comfortable to move. Finally, he could stand it no longer and, accompanied by some wisecracks from the rest of us nicely tucked up in bed, made his way outside. Soon after, I heard water dripping from a tin can. This continued until everybody was resisting the call. The dripping water? It was Fred lying in bed and pouring water from one can to another. When Fred can't sleep...

One weekend Fred decided to landscape the 'box' and planted a little willow by the door. Fred loved that willow; every weekend he tended it with loving care. Several weeks later Peter Drennan came with me again. He was little more than a boy and very helpful.

Fred and I were fishing when Pete appeared. 'I've been tidying up Fred,' Peter said. 'I've cut the grass, mended the gate and – oh yes, removed that willow which was obstructing the door.'

Fred did his nut again.

Yes, we had our laughs all right. One night Joe thought he saw a ghost. Suddenly awakened, he opened his eyes and looked towards the open doorway. In the light of the moon Joe could see a white figure standing at the door. Joe let out a little scream and leapt out of bed. As he did so the figure turned round – Fred standing in his vest and pants was admiring the night sky. Poor Joe!

Tag Barnes came down for a weekend. Nobody was there when he arrived, so he decided to fish the lake. Fred eventually arrived and decided to frighten Tag. Immediately behind Tag was a bush and, creeping up behind it, Fred removed every stitch of his clothing then crept up on the unsuspecting Tag, tapped him on the back and jumped head-first over his shoulder into his swim. Poor Tag!

In between all these goings-on we caught fish, and I always mentioned the fact I was 'the greatest'. One bitterly cold day everybody had forsaken the river in favour of the lake but nothing was doing and Joe said, 'What a lousy lot of fishermen we are!'

'What do you mean?' I said, 'I could catch a chub if I wanted to – and be back in five minutes.'

'Bet you can't,' said Joe, 'bet you a pound.'

I gathered my tackle whilst the others checked their watches. Somebody, I think, blew a whistle, and I shot off at top speed to a swim 300 yards upstream. Leaning over a barbed-wire fence I teased my bait under a bush; the rod tip trembled, I stuck – and bingo! I slipped the net under the fence, unhooked the chub, passed the line back over the fence, then, with the fish in my net ran back as fast as I could.

'Stoney's got one,' I heard Ken say. I placed the chub at Joe's feet.

'How's that?' I said. 'Four and a half minutes dead.'

I might have known...

'You're late,' five voices said in unison. 'A minute over time, you've lost.' I never got my quid.

One night I accidentally left my rod at the river with a dead-bait attached. Next morning at dawn I found I had had a 'run'. 'Ah,' I thought, 'a big eel.' I then discovered that exactly five yards of line remained on the spool which the previous evening I had loaded with 200 yards of 12-lb. monofil. For 150 yards downstream the bank was lined with hawthorns with gaps between. And my line was pointing under them.

I walked down to the first bush, cut the line, walked round the other side and retied it. Then to the next bush, cut, retie, to the next bush, and so on. And my new line... well, it just wasn't new any more. Half an hour and 195 yards of line later I reached the end – this was it. Against the bank was a high raft of weed which, with some difficulty, I pulled ashore. In the middle, wrapped around my tackle, was a 12-inch pike!

Which reminds me. One day I badly hooked a jack and killed it. As there appeared to be something big inside I slit it open then tossed it back into the river. Shortly afterwards Joe, who had been fishing further downstream, came along.

'Did you see that little Johnny Jack Pike?' Joe said. 'Well,

it floated past me and I said 'Good Morning Mr Pike, and how are you this morning?' 'A bit rough,' he replied – 'stomach trouble – can't keep a thing down.'
Yes, we had lots of fun in and around that 'box'.

Six years have now passed since I last fished Theale. But I'm not complaining, for I spent seven very happy years fishing the lake, canal and river. That enormous barbel inhabit the river there is little doubt, but it was one of those waters where the size didn't matter; it was 'Fun Fishing' – with a capital 'F'.

3. Snowberry Lake

In 1965, Fred Taylor was offered the lease on a small Buckinghamshire pit. Set in private grounds, little more than two acres in extent and completely surrounded with trees, it was not only picturesque but unique, insomuch that, apart from some marginal rushes, it was completely free of weed. Much of the lake was unfishable due to hawthorn and other bushes which overhung its banks; it was, without doubt, one of the nicest waters I have seen.

Before taking an option on the lease Fred decided he would like to fish it, and during the close season obtained permission from the river authority to do so. One afternoon he strolled down to the lake and cast out a large lob close to the boathouse. As it sank the float slid under. A minute later Fred netted a monster perch weighing $4\frac{1}{4}$ lb. He decided to take the option!

Little did we know it then, but that perch was typical of the pattern of events which were to follow. Subsequent visits proved that the fish were either 'on' or 'off' – most times I fished they were 'off'! Most of the perch (and very few of them) were caught immediately on arrival; if you didn't catch one in the first hour then your chances were poor. But when you did catch one it was worth all the frustration. In the first season Dick Walker took two 4-lb. perch plus another smaller fish. Other members also caught odd fish in excess of 3 lb.

Besides perch the lake also held carp, tench, bream and zander. The carp were not very large but the tench were – five pounds and over. The zander were mostly small with the odd good one. That, as far as we knew, was all the lake held. Until one night in July, that is.

Fred Towns and I arrived one Friday evening having planned an all-night session. Not that I expected to catch a perch after dark, but there was a good chance of one at dusk or first light. During the hours between – 10 p.m. and 3 a.m. – I would keep watch over a lob just in case a big tench came along. Conditions were good, an overcast sky and the air warm. All it wanted was a bite from a big fish.

The evening (as usual) passed without incident. As darkness came I inspected and re-cast my lob, put the rod between two rests and settled down for the night with Fred fishing alongside.

The lake, which by day was so picturesque, now took on a different atmosphere. Owls hooted above us and strange cries came from beyond. Fred and I watched the tackle intently, but our lines remained hanging loosely from the rod tops.

It was nearing midnight when I noticed the reel handle turning; somehow I had forgotten to lift the pick-up. I picked up the rod and struck. On feeling the hook the fish made off slowly but determinedly. I piled on all the pressure I dared, but you can't put too much on a 6-lb. b.s. line and it was impossible to prevent line from being taken. Although difficult to judge at night, I hazard a guess that quite 20 yards of line were taken from me before the fish stopped running. I knew I was into a heavy fish.

But what was it? Perch no, even if I had copped one feeding at night, there just couldn't be a perch this big. Tench – possibly; if so, I could well have a record fish. The most feasible explanation was carp, yet the fight (and it *was* a fight) didn't add up to carp. If only the hook would hold . . .

Slowly, very slowly, I gained line until the fish was within reach. Five or six minutes had now passed and I still didn't know what it was. But we soon would for Fred had now dipped the large landing net into the water and Fred doesn't make many mistakes. I saw the fish wallow just beyond the net and asked Fred to shine the torch. As it did so a large pair of whiskers appeared above the surface – catfish! Seconds later Fred slipped the net under three feet of wriggling fish and lifted it out on to the bank.

I had never seen a 'cat' before and believe me it isn't a pleasant sight at night. Not only that, but I had considerable difficulty in holding the blessed thing, for that mouth looked very wicked to me. I removed the hook and slipped the fish into my outsize keepnet ready for weighing next morning. I don't know when a fish has shaken me more; it wasn't so much the sight of it but the unexpectedness of it all.

Next morning the scales showed the fish at 12 lb., and after pictures had been taken it was returned to the water.

The following Saturday we went there again. We arrived at tea-time having planned another all-night session. It was scorching hot and as we approached the boathouse we witnessed a sight we had not seen before or since. An area of water several feet across was the colour of mustard, with rubbish galore being thrown up from the bottom. 'Um', I said to Fred, 'I'll fish there later on.' Later on, indeed; why I didn't fish it there and then I shall never know. When I did return, of course, the disturbance had ceased – the fish were gone. Carp or catfish? We shall never know, but what an opportunity wasted!

I fished the lake on and off for three years. My ambition at that time was the capture of a monster perch – an ambition still to be fulfilled. For despite repeated visits – both by day and night – I didn't succeed in hooking one. One hot summer morning two large perch came cruising past under a hawthorn bush, but those were the only perch I ever saw – either in or out of the water. One evening I did hook a big fish which came unstuck – what it was I don't know – but that, and the 'cat' were the only decent fish I ever hooked there.

Trouble was – at least as far as the perch were concerned – this business of catching them immediately you started fishing. It was either that or nothing. In effect then, after an hour you usually knew your fate, and because of that I didn't like 'wasting' a full day's fishing there. And with a round trip of 80 miles, weekday evenings – when I catch the bulk of my best fish – were 'out'. With better and more consistent fishing available much nearer home I finally opted out of the syndicate.

And there's a story in that too. The chap who took my permit wanted very badly to catch a big perch. The first time he went he took Ken Taylor along. 'Have a go in there,' Ken said (where my 'cat' had come from) 'you will probably catch a three-pounder.' He did too – before Ken could tackle up!

During the course of a season I fish a wide variety of waters in different parts of the country. Each water has its problems of course – what would fishing be without them – but none more so than that little lake. It gives its fish up grudgingly. Only Dick Walker has taken more than two fish, and his total is only three!

Every time I wound my way back through the hawthorns, past the weeping willows and under the silver birches, I could almost hear a sense of defiance coming from the water. A mysterious place indeed.

4. The swing to the sea

In the summer of 1962 Fred Taylor, three others and I spent a week at Fowey, sea fishing. For me it was something of an adventure for I had never been to sea before, at least not to fish; now I was going to spend a full week at it. The boats had been booked, and the skipper was very experienced. All it wanted was good weather.

We put to sea on the Sunday morning with a supply of live sand-eels on board. Our quarry was pollack, for which Cornwall is justifiably famous. Soon we had passed the estuary mouth and out into the open sea.

On the journey out the skipper informed us that a number of basking sharks were in the vicinity. 'Are they harmless?' I asked. 'Oh yes,' John replied, 'but don't take them for granted, should one get under the boat and surface, well...' Nevertheless, I thought it would be nice if I could get some close-up pictures. 'We'll see,' said John. 'I'll keep my eyes open for them.'

The marks were still two miles distant when a shout from John had us looking in the direction in which he was pointing. There, less than 200 yards ahead, several large black dorsal fins moved slowly towards the boat. Although the obvious course was to steer the boat away from the huge creatures, we decided otherwise, for here was a great chance to photograph them at close range. The engines were cut and, with my camera at the ready, we slowly cruised towards them.

Less than 20 yards now separated us, and already those large fins looked menacing. Seconds later we were alongside the nearest shark, so close in fact that the boatman reached over and touched it. Then, slowly, the giant fish turned away and disappeared from view.

THE SWING TO THE SEA

Now the engines were roaring again for it was time to make a hasty retreat. Basking sharks (which live entirely on plankton) have a habit of leaping clear of the water, and in doing so could easily capsize a 22-ft. boat such as ours. We had not travelled 100 yards when one of these giants cleared the water by several feet, falling back again with a splash which had to be seen to be believed. I make no bones of the fact that I was very relieved to leave them behind.

How big were they? I hesitate to say, but the fish John touched was the length of the boat and quite five feet across. John estimated it not far short of two tons.

An hour later the echo sounder picked up a vast shoal of fish close to the bottom. Tackle was quickly assembled and it was then that I learnt something about pollack fishing – the importance of depth. We paid out line until the lead touched bottom then made one turn of the reel; a wait of ten seconds, then another turn, and so on until a fish took. By this time the number of turns had been noted and the rest was easy; wait for the bait to settle, then make the required number of turns – and bingo! We returned that evening with the hold full of pollack – fish between five and ten pounds. An exciting day with fish coming to the net fast and furious providing, of course, one gave the required number of turns. In this case it had been 12; to give less meant no bites. Strange that a foot should make all the difference in that vast sea. But it's true.

That week at Fowey – a week in which we took dozens of pollack, bass and conger – my interest in sea fishing increased. I enquired as to whether good shore fishing was available. 'Yes,' said John, 'try off the big flat rock alongside the railway – plenty of conger there. Fish at night on the high tide and you can't fail.' Fred, Brian and I decided to give them a try, and one evening, having caught some mackerel for bait, made our way down to the rock.

Mugs that we were, we had not come prepared for conger. 'But there,' I said to Fred, 'I should like to see *any* fish beat me on a S/U Mark IV and 15-lb. b.s. line.' 15 lb. you know! As I said, we knew nothing about sea fishing . . .

COME FISHING WITH ME

We tackled up, placed half a mackerel on a 6/o hook (I think it was a 6/o – anyway it looked b...huge to me!) cast our baits about fifteen yards out from the rock, then settled down for our all-night vigil.

Or at least I did. The day had been hot and Fred and Brian asked whether I would mind being watchdog whilst they went for a pint, with a promise to return before nightfall. They had been gone some time, and it was now dark, the stillness of the night broken only by the waves beating against the rocks below. Further up the estuary faint voices could be heard coming from the pubs in town. Giant cargo ships, their shapes barely discernible, looked eerie across the water. The tide was making fast; soon it would have reached its top, stopping a foot or so below the rock on which I was sitting. A mumbling, singing, drunk passed by thirty feet up along the old disused track, otherwise I was alone. There was an atmosphere about the place, and I was a little uneasy.

Suddenly one of the rods clattered against the rock. Shining the torch I could see the reel gently turning. Conger! But that was not all; the reels on the other rods were also turning. The situation had become frightening; to be alone with one conger in such circumstances was bad enough – but three! If they took sufficient line – and I didn't know how much Fred and Brian had – the rods would surely disappear. I had to think fast and line was streaming off my reel. I slammed the reel into gear, waited for the fish to tighten and struck. To my surprise the conger kept going; my gear was useless. Applying pressure the rod slowly bent until the line suddenly parted with an almighty 'crack'. The rod straightened and he was gone.

But the other rods; the reels were still turning – where in the dickens were Fred and Brian? Grabbing the rod nearest to me I hit the fish which again just kept going – but not for long. Again the tackle was inadequate – and I was powerless. Eventually the line parted.

Brian's gear proved a little better, and I did in fact turn the conger. 'Pumping' as hard as I could I gained ground, but it wasn't easy – a conger fifty yards or more out from the shore takes some holding. Suddenly all went solid – the conger no doubt having taken refuge under a rock. I didn't see that tackle again!

Ten minutes later the others returned. I related my story whilst Fred, eager to fish, tackled up again. I watched him cast, hoping he would get a run, but time was running out, for the tide was ebbing fast and soon it would be too late.

Suddenly Fred was away. I watched his reel turning as the conger made for its favourite rock then, with thirty feet of line gone, Fred struck. The conger surprisingly gave ground, and provided only token resistance until directly under the rock; then all went solid. Occasionally the rod would pull over, a sign the fish was still there. For ten minutes it was stalemate; suddenly we realised the sea was no longer pounding the rock. Something strange was amiss.

Shining my powerful torch we were astonished to see the bottom of the rock on dry land – the sea was at full ebb. Thirty feet below, the beam picked out a rock situated a few feet from the one on which we were standing. Protruding from the smaller rock was the head of Fred's conger still attached to the line – no wonder he couldn't move it!

Fred suggested breaking but I said no, yet the situation looked impossible; Fred had only to slacken off slightly for the eel to disappear completely. I then had an idea. Brian had brought back some beer and one bottle was empty. I asked Fred whether he thought he could drop the bottle on the eel's head whilst Brian shone the torch. Fred asked why but I told him not to ask questions and took his rod. I applied pressure and the eel's head came into view. Fred dropped the bottle bang on target; the eel relaxed its grip, and I hauled it up the rock face. Ten pounds it weighed. What you might call 'fun fishing' (but not for the eel).

I returned home a confirmed sea angler despite one day (well, an hour really) spent at sea during a gale. Rough weather had kept us inside, but with a conger trip planned that evening and no fresh bait available I thought it would be a good idea to poke our noses out and catch a few. Fred, Brian and the boatman tried to dissuade me but, under pressure, agreed to go. Never again shall I 'pressurise' a boatman. Once outside the estuary mouth, the boat did everything but turn over and John, urged on by Fred and Brian, went further and further out. (Of course John knew it was all right, otherwise he would never have gone, but I didn't think of that at the time.) I was soaked from water coming over the boat; I stumbled, fell over, yet I wasn't scared. I was bloody well terrified! And all the time Fred sat at the other end laughing his head off and saying 'Further out John, Stoney *must* have his mackerel.'

It was the only time in my life when I felt like smacking Fred round the ear but there was no chance of that – I was too busy trying to prevent myself from going overboard. Never have I been so glad to get back on 'terra firma' as I was that evening.

Several years later Joe Taylor and I spent a fortnight with Bill Warren fishing the Avon. One morning Bill came down to say he had booked a boat to fish off the Needles; would we care to go? I didn't need asking twice, especially as the boatman was highly respected in that area.

It was a beautiful sunny morning as we left Mudeford Quay, the sea a flat calm. After half an hour steaming we arrived at the mark and dropped anchor. We had no gear, but Ted Harding, the boatman, fixed us up and we were soon fishing with half a mackerel lying on the bottom. I removed my pullover, and laying the rod against the gunwale (with all tension on the reel removed), I sat back to enjoy the sun.

Suddenly, without warning, my peace was disturbed. We were discussing prospects when the check on the reel started to scream. Hastily I grabbed the rod (tied to the boat for safety), released the check, and with one finger lightly on the rim of the centre-pin allowed the fish to run. With incredible speed line was stripped from the reel then, with almost 70 yards out, it stopped. But not for long – ten seconds maybe – then it was off again. I adjusted the tension, tightened on the running fish, and hit him. Five or six minutes later the fish was alongside and Ted, with not a little skill, lifted my first tope aboard, a fish of 35 lb.

More and more coarse fishermen are turning to sea fishing. This has, in many cases, led to better techniques and finer tackle being used, for there is little doubt that on suitable tackle most sea fish can give a very fine account of themselves indeed – better than most coarse fish.

Sea anglers, don't get me wrong! There are, I know, many knowledgeable sea fishermen (men like Clive Gammon have preached this gospel for years), but I think it is fair to say that many anglers fish with tackle that is far too heavy for the job in hand. The result of this, of course, is that little, if any, fight is produced by the fish, which is a pity.

After the capture of my first tope I realised that I could use much finer gear. On my next trip I took along a 10-ft. glass rod with a 2½ lb. test curve which I had built for the job, a centre-pin reel with 300 yards of 20-lb. b.s. line attached. I would have preferred a finer line to this – 15-lb. b.s. say – but because of the hook size (I think now they were too large) necessary to hold the bait it would not set the hook at long distances. Anyway this is my tope outfit, and believe me, a tope on that tackle will give you very fine sport indeed.

Ted Harding taught me much about sea fishing, including the actual boating of a tope. He doesn't believe in gaffing tope and I quite agree; far more exciting to lift them by hand – and cleaner too. After seeing Ted lift my first tope into the boat I had to have a go. As I said, it's exciting. Now, unless I consider pictures more important, I do the job myself.

Once the tope is alongside, take hold of it just above the tail and, with the other hand, catch hold of its dorsal fin; then, with a quick lift, bring it into the boat. The operation may appear a little risky but keep a cool head and it is safe enough. The fish will thrash about a bit and you get a little damp but it's all in the fun. Don't panic or drop the fish; that's important.

On one occasion we came very near to catching a great haul of tope. Peter Drennan, Ian Tolputt, Joe Taylor and I were aboard, but before we could drop anchor a storm blew up.

Anyhow, Ted put the anchor down bang on the spot and we started fishing. The rain was belting down, and Ian was already sea sick. Peter didn't look too well either, but he was soon into a tope. By now Ian was really ill, and in an effort to 'revive' him I thrust a rod into his hand with a tope attached. Even that failed to interest him. By this time, Joe was sitting in one corner eating sandwiches, and passing them round to poor old Pete and Ian saying 'have a sandwich?'. Peter, too, was now very ill, and with me well on the way we decided to pack. We had only been fishing an hour but four good tope were aboard – all, funnily enough, taken on one side of the boat. If only we could have stayed...

For several years after that I fished with Ted and caught many tope – plus other species of course. One year my wife badgered me into taking her along too, so, the following summer I fixed a date.

Now I've always made it a rule never to give my rod over to anyone until I know what is on the end. That day I broke my rule, and it cost me a good fish.

As on my first trip, it was a gloriously hot day, the sea a 'flat calm'. Having anchored, I decided to go for tope, and whilst I fixed the tope gear Sue busied herself catching mackerel for bait. Ten minutes later, with several in the bait box, I lowered a fillet overboard, hoping one would smell it out.

I didn't wait long. Suddenly the reel screamed as a tope bolted with the bait then, with over 100 yards between me and the fish, I struck. On my light freshwater tackle the tope took some stopping, and it was quite fifteen minutes before I had him alongside. The scales stopped at 35 lb. Sue by this time was at the other end of the boat; clearly she didn't like tope!

I caught two more good fish, plus a nice skate, when Sue said, 'I'd like to catch something – but not a tope.' 'All right,' I replied, 'if a skate picks up my bait you catch it.' Five minutes later I had a bite.

Several short pulls, then the long, steady, downward pull. I struck. All went solid. I then felt the fish move, and, applying pressure, shifted him off the bottom. I thrust the rod into Sue's hands and said 'There's your skate, now land it'.

Five minutes later she was still struggling – and we hadn't even seen the fish. I looked at Sue leaning backwards battling with a fish which was refusing to give line. 'Come on,' I said, 'give it some stick, about time you landed the blessed thing.' 'I can't,' Sue replied, puffing and blowing, the reel screaming as the fish made another plunge towards the bottom.

Five minutes later I got a glimpse of a large ugly black creature. 'Monkfish,' I shouted, and grabbing the camera started to reel off pictures as the fish lunged and rolled beneath the surface, the lens (covered with a clear filter) less than two feet from the surface. As the fish surfaced Ted plunged in the gaff, a heave and over the gunwhale it came. With water flying everywhere I took shots from every angle, shots the like of which I might not get again. One quick blow on the head silenced the 'Monk' and Ted hoisted it on to the balance. The needle stopped at 40 lb.!

Although I was pleased for Sue, I couldn't help feeling just a little choked, but there, I had some wonderful shots and I opened the camera to remove the film. But somehow, during loading, the film had failed to engage on the spool. There were no pictures; just a blank film.

5. Blenheim Lake

Blenheim Palace is known the world over. Every year thousands of visitors pass through its gates to look over the home of the Duke of Marlborough and where, in 1874, Winston Churchill was born. In the grounds pheasants run wild (or should I say tame), while the surrounding lakes are inhabited by hundreds of duck and other water fowl. And big pike.

I first fished Blenheim in 1962. I remember the occasion quite clearly; a beautiful sunny, November day, with the copper beech trees making a perfect setting. It was shortly after dawn that we rowed out from the boathouse and made our way towards the dam. Here, the water is deep, with tree roots reaching out into the lake – ideal pike 'country'.

The morning passed quietly. We caught several pike, biggest 10 lb., but not one of the leviathans we knew were there. Midday came and the sun shone through from a cloudless sky. Then suddenly it happened. A shoal of roach, hundreds strong, suddenly leapt from the water. At the same time, several pike, two certainly 20 lb., possibly more, half-rolled, half-leapt among the roach. A minute later the roach (most of which were over a pound with many topping two pounds) 'showered' again, this time further along the lake. Soon after, another leaping shoal joined the first, then another, until the surface of the lake for over 100 yards was a turmoil of leaping roach and crashing pike. One massive fish cleared the water close to our boat, the waves eventually reaching the far bank.

It is impossible to describe on paper the sight of those leaping roach. Imagine hundreds of bleak attacking a crust then, as a predator strikes, scattering in all directions. In chapter 8 I have described this occurrence which takes place when bream are feeding. Substitute pound roach for the bleak, and you have the idea.

That afternoon we caught twenty-two pike, best 16 lb., all caught on live-baits fished close to the bottom; yes, that's what I said, 'close to the bottom'. What fools we were: those pike were surface feeding, and that's where our baits should have been, not on the bottom. I didn't try a wobbled dead bait, nor a spinner or plug – why I shall never know.

Shortly after that harrowing experience, the local aquadivers contacted me. They had apparently 'dived' Blenheim many times and had sighted several very large pike. They suggested a plan; they would come fishing with us and dive, then, if they sighted a big 'un would guide us to him. Unsporting? Maybe. Interesting? definitely!

The date was fixed for one January – yes January! – morning and we met at the dam. We had been fishing for three or four hours when they arrived and told them that no one had had an offer. This didn't surprise them one little bit for they had never seen a pike in that particular area. And so it proved that morning; no pike were sighted, and none were caught.

But they did have some interesting observations to make. They pointed out an area where large pike had been seen, a patch of water in the middle where the bottom contours were very uneven. The following week I copped an eighteen-pounder there and two weeks later a friend, John Bremner, caught two, 18 lb. and 21 lb. We decided to concentrate on this obvious 'hot-spot', and by lining the boat up so that a silver birch tree was in the centre of the boat and a litter basket level with one end I was able to anchor right where the pike were. It was, we thought, merely a matter of time before one of us copped a really big 'un.

After several visits Fred Towns and I decided that trolling was probably the best method of catching those Blenheim pike. Here, the oarsman (usually me!) plays a vital rôle; that of keeping the boat moving at *just* the right speed. Over deep water the stroke rate is lowered; as the deeps meet the shallows the rate is increased. In cold weather the boat must move as slowly as possible – not always easy, especially in gale force winds and we fished in plenty of those.

A bite is signalled by the clutch, set loosely, screaming. The oarsman stops rowing and drops one anchor, while his companion takes the rod. Good fun but hard – and often, cold – work.

Of course, trolling is not new, and I had fished the method before with fair success. In the past, though, I have trolled with the bait fished deep and this I think is a mistake. Let me explain.

Blenheim consists of deeps and shallows with heavy weed growth rising well off the bottom even in winter. Some days the pike are on the shallows, on others in the deeps. So we fish until we find them. With the bait set too deep this can take a long time.

At the beginning, Fred and I fished our baits – live ones – about six feet below the float trailing some 20 yards or so behind the boat. Trouble was, many false runs occurred due to the bait fouling the weed. Then came the job of dropping the oars, retrieving the bait and starting all over again. It was a frustrating – and time-wasting – business.

We eventually decided to fish with the baits set much higher in the water – 3 ft. or so. Pulling out from the boathouse one morning we made tracks for a 'hot-spot', but apart from two small fish it proved fruitless. Gently pulling on the oars I made for some shallow water, for I had a hunch we would find them there.

We had travelled about 200 yards when Fred's rod pulled over. I stopped the boat and watched. A false alarm again, the bait festooned with weed. The floats were then pushed down to within 2 ft. of the bait and gently pulling on the oars I made a straight line parallel to the bank.

Suddenly Fred was away. Holding the boat steady I watched him tighten on the fish and strike. A nice fish – 10 lb. exactly.

On the third pull of the oars Fred's rod pulled over again. I decided on some action shots and reached for the camera. Ever tried holding the net with one hand and taking shots with the other? Anyway, I got my pictures and netted the fish through the viewfinder! It was 14 lb.

Now it was my turn and I caught two fish in quick succession. But our bait supply was running out – at least as far as bream and roach were concerned – but Fred had taken his fish on dead ones, so deadbait it was. Turning the boat round I took a second run along the bank, further out this time.

But a gale-force wind hampered progress, and we decided to anchor for a while. Against a patch of rushes a fish swirled and I quickly placed a live bleak in the spot. It didn't stay long and I had him – another ten-pounder. A smaller fish followed, then nothing.

The keepnet was now crowded and we decided to release the fish. A short row to the bank, some pictures, then off again. Rowing was easier, and we were soon watching our floats trailing well behind the boat.

For a time all was quiet but suddenly my rod pulled over. I dropped the oars and opened the pick-up. No 'knocking' was taking place – this I liked – just a slow, steady run. After a very good scrap I had him alongside and Fred slid him into the net, a short thick fish of 17 lb.

It was nearly dark, just time for one more row along the shallows. One more fish fell to my rod – a hard-fighting fish of 9 lb. – and that was that. More picture taking, then the long, hard row back to the boathouse.

Where bottom weed is prolific a bait fished high in the water appears most successful. Percy Silman, head bailiff at Blenheim, catches his pike with metal spoons and when spinning at Blenheim you must spin high in the water to clear the weed – from the bank that is. The two factors appear to tie with one another.

Fred and I also discovered that it didn't matter whether the bait was dead or alive. In fact they might well be more effective when fished dead. We didn't bother with fancy rigs, merely lip-hooking the bait through the top lip. I like a float – a small piece of cork actually – which prevents the bait from sinking too deep and resulting in false bites. Certainly the presence of a float didn't appear to scare the pike. The extra movement (and consequent vibration) could even be an added advantage.

During the next two years I fished Blenheim many times and took my share of good pike. But not once did I see those leviathans I had seen chasing the roach. Not until 1969 that is.

Between us, Fred and I have taken many nice pike at Blenheim but at the time of writing I have yet to take a 'twenty'. I feel I have been a trifle unlucky here for I have seen several caught – often by very inexperienced anglers. And Fred copped one the very first time he fished there. Its capture – and subsequent events – are worth relating.

The event took place roughly twelve months after we met and Fred confided in me that he had never caught a double-figure pike. And he wanted one – badly. That day our Specimen Group came along and as the boats pulled out from the boathouse I jokingly remarked to the other boats 'Towns is on a beating today; doesn't know a thing about pike fishing'. Fred remained silent; afterwards I wished I had.

I rowed the boat out to the spot where I had taken several good pike, the swim in fact, which the aqua divers had suggested. We decided to anchor and tackled up with identical rigs, each with a live-bait attached. We made our first casts and our baits landed no more than ten feet apart. Both floats disappeared immediately and seconds later we were both into pike. Mine was a small one and was quickly boated, but Fred was into something good. With camera round my neck and landing net at the ready I watched Fred do battle.

The fish indulged in a series of short hard runs and it was quite three minutes before I saw the pike four feet down. 'For heaven's sake be careful,' I said, 'it's certainly twenty, might well be thirty.' Two minutes later the pike surfaced and Fred pulled it over my waiting net. A quick lift and over he came – the biggest pike I had ever netted.

Because of its size we up-anchored and rowed to the bank at the Grand Bridge for weighing and photographs. The scales stopped at $27\frac{1}{2}$ lb. I took some shots, then Fred returned it to the water. Oh, the ribbing I endured; why hadn't I kept my big mouth shut?

Our final trip that season was in March. Soon after we started Fred took a seventeen-pounder but at tea-time it was our only fish. 'Let's give that area a try where you copped your big one,' I said, 'perhaps we will catch it again.' I had to agree with Fred, however, that the possibility of the fish having found its way back from the bridge was remote, and the chances of catching it again were almost nil. Still we would try.

I lined the boat up with the two landmarks so we were bang on target. We both put live-baits out, again close together. 'If he is about, Fred,' I said, 'I might draw him to us.' On my second rod I mounted a herring and cast it beyond our live-baits, gently 'wobbling' it back between them. I repeated this performance quite twenty times but with no response. 'Come on,' I said, 'let's go!' I wound in my live-bait, Fred picked up his rod, turned the handle once, then stopped. 'Something has grabbed it,' he said. My herring had done its job.

The fight was not a spectacular one. As the pike surfaced we could see it was the same fish taken four months earlier: a fish which now looked old and, I think, nearing death. We checked its weight – four ounces lighter this time – and slipped it back. We would like to think it survived, but I doubt it.

That pike had travelled over 300 yards through dense weed to find its original lie. To catch it twice in that vast water was remarkable.

The following year I was asked to catch a pike for the television cameras. We couldn't have chosen a worse day. Two days continuous rain had flooded the nearby river Glyne which flows into the lake, consequently the water was heavily coloured. And it was bitterly cold. Trying to catch a pike wouldn't be easy, and so it proved. I tried live-baits at anchor; big, flashy spinners fished slowly, and wobbled dead baits – all to no avail. Time was running out and I was cold – not to mention the camera team. 'I'll give the area towards the dam a troll,' I said, 'might be lucky and find one.'

On the third run down the clutch suddenly screamed out;

I dropped the oars and took the rod. The line moved gently through my fingers – always the sign of a good fish. I waited a few seconds, then drove the hook home. Two minutes later I caught a glimpse of a large broad back, and soon after I pulled him over the net – 16 lb. With the fish 'in the can' and fingers numbed we packed. I worked hard for that one.

Over the years we have learnt a bit about Blenheim, its pike, and the best ways of catching them. I have fished there in all sorts of conditions; hot, cloudless, summer days, in gale-force winds, pouring rain and, on one occasion, through the ice. That day the Group arrived to find the lake completely frozen with just one small clear area in the middle. We made it, by one man standing at the front of the boat and rocking it furiously whilst the other kept the broken ice away from the sides. How I sweated despite the cold. Fish? We never had a bite!

In general, one noticeable feature has been the success of small baits – especially bleak. One day, however, I decided to leave the small baits at home and took along the biggest herrings I could buy – many of which topped the pound. All day I 'wobbled' them in all the 'hot-spots' – and took pike from almost every one. The best pike just about made 5 lb., the smallest, well ... it was smaller than the herring!

The last time I fished Blenheim the ground was covered with snow, the margins of the lake fringed with ice. Pheasants called in the woods beyond and, as darkness fell, hordes of duck came in from the tree tops. The last of the visitors filed over the Grand Bridge, lights in the Palace were turned on. We rowed back to the boathouse over the area where a few years earlier we had witnessed the crashing pike as they harassed the roach shoals. Now all was quiet; we broke down our tackle, cleaned the boat and trudged wearily up the hill. As we reached the top we looked down at the water glistening in the moonlight; a cold, cheerless water. I dream of the day when I see an enormous head with jaws large enough to swallow the resident coots and ducks come sliding over the gunwale – on my tackle!

6. The Upper Ouse

In November 1958 the Group fished Dick Walker's reach of the Upper Ouse at Beachampton. Very few fish were caught which, in view of the conditions, was not surprising, but that didn't matter; we were fishing a water renowned for its monster chub. Shortly after, Dick very kindly gave me permission to fish there as often as I wanted to, and to take whom I liked. It was a generous gesture, which I not only appreciated but also decided to take advantage of. That season I paid several visits to the water and saw some very large fish – especially chub. But they were difficult fish; in fact Dick told me that if I had one bite a day I would do well; if I actually caught chub, well... I'd had a good day! 'But,' Dick told me, 'if you do catch one it's more likely to be five pounds than four.' So I fished Beachampton as much as I could, but those chub – at least the five-pounders – proved very elusive.

My first Beachampton chub weighed $4\frac{1}{2}$ lb. – my only bite that day. Shortly after, the magazine *Angling* ran a competition for boys, the prize being a day out with Fred J. Taylor, Ken Mansfield the Editor, and myself. During the afternoon I wandered off upstream to see if I could catch a chub. Sliding down the bank on my stomach I got into position and cast into a 'hot-spot' between two beds of bulrushes. The rod top moved – just – but enough. Four-and-a-half pounds he weighed, and the boys were pleased. So was I, but it wasn't the 'fiver' I wanted.

In subsequent visits I took several four-pounders – but no 'fives'. It *was* difficult fishing with, on average, one bite a day, but I didn't mind that so much; trouble was, the 'gremlins' were at work. They were turning five-pound chub into four-pounders once I hooked them!

But if I couldn't catch five-pounders, Joe Taylor certainly could. In Joe I saw my answer. Yes, of course he would put me into one; we arranged to meet one Saturday in February.

The morning was cold as I arrived at the river, and whilst we were walking to our swims snow began to fall. I wasn't worried, however, for snow storms had, in the past, proved lucky for me. The river was in perfect order; all I wanted was the right fish to bite.

We eventually arrived at our swim. A small willow leaned into the river against the far bank and just upstream of this was a bed of bulrushes. Joe dropped his gear and issued instructions. The 'hot-spot' he said, was in midstream, two feet upstream of the willow: if I cast anywhere else I would not get a bite. He then said something that filled me with excitement. 'Very rarely,' he said, 'is a chub taken from that swim *under* five pounds, and if you fish carefully you should get one.' With that he walked off, leaving me to it.

I tackled up with a 6-lb. b.s. line and a ½-oz. Arlesey Bomb stopped two inches from a No. 8 hook. On this I attached a small piece of crust and, creeping down the bank, I got into position.

Carefully I cast to the off side of the 'hot spot' and allowed my bait to roll into position. Half an hour passed without incident; then, suddenly the rod top kicked back slightly, no more than an inch. I struck, and a heavy fish moved towards the bush. I held him hard, and gradually worked him towards me. I knew it was a good fish and when he finally broke surface, Joe, who by this time had arrived, said 'five pounds'. Another dash towards the rushes beat him, and into the net he went.

I carried him up the bank to weigh – so I hoped – my first five-pounder. But I was doomed to disappointment; 4 lb. 14 oz. the balance read and no amount of juggling – and believe me I *did* juggle! – would take it over the magic five. It was, I admit, an anti-climax, and no one was more sorry than Joe. 'You must be very unlucky,' he said, 'they always weigh five pounds from this swim.' He then reassured me, if only slightly. 'Sometimes,' he said, 'but not often I admit, you catch two here, and when you do it is *always* a five pounder; never known it otherwise.'

Even so, I decided to rest the swim and fish it later in the day. Several hours later, having added nothing to the bag, I returned and took up position again.

Almost immediately the rod top moved forward an inch or so; I struck, and again a heavy fish moved towards the bank. I could hardly believe it – a five-pounder at last. But as I took it from the net I had my doubts – 12 oz. short. I looked at Joe. 'You *are* unlucky,' he said, 'never known that before.' We took some pictures and, with the snow still beating down, we packed.

The following year, still not having taken a five-pounder from that river, I fished it again, this time higher up. By a coincidence it snowed that day too, but the river was in good order. Ian Tolputt accompanied me, and we chose a swim where a number of five-pounders are taken each season. I had on several occasions fished this swim, and although I had never taken a chub from there, this time I was confident.

The first cast I was into one. The bite was most difficult to detect and could so easily have been mistaken for the current shifting the lead. But it wasn't, and here I was playing a heavy chub. I got him out all right, but again the balance told a sad story – 4 lb. 10 oz. This must, I thought be my one and only chance, for only on very rare occasions do you get two chub from the same hole on this reach.

Before I could cast however, Ian, who was fishing the same swim, hooked one. 'How odd,' I thought, 'if Ian on this, his first visit, should catch a five-pounder.' Alas no, but a good fish nevertheless – 4½ lb.

Minutes later he hooked yet another. As I lifted the net for him I thought 'this one must break the barrier'. Not quite though – 4 lb. 14 oz. – oh, what rotten luck. Three fish from one swim was far more than we expected and, not surprisingly, the bites ceased.

I then decided to move to a heavily-fished pool close to the road. Although the pool is deep it is difficult to approach, and I am always afraid I have been spotted before I start fishing, for the bank is high and steep. But its inhabitants are large, and here, I thought, with the fish feeding like this, I stood a wonderful chance.

I could hardly believe my eyes when, minutes after casting, the rod top moved. I hooked him, and instead of tearing off as usual this one bored deeply. After a while I surfaced him and breathed a sigh of relief – this *must* be five pounds and triumphantly I carried him up the bank. Then I had doubts. This chub, although much bigger than the others, was a 'twicer', for it had a 'keepnet' tail. My fears were confirmed when the balance stopped at 4 lb 10 oz. That fish should, without doubt, have been a five-pounder.

I have often been asked whether luck enters into fishing. I don't deny that you must have luck, but it plays a very small part, and the angler who relies on luck alone will not be successful very often. I've experienced days when I could do nothing wrong; on the other hand, I've had many days when I felt that even the smallest slice had deserted me.

I have described two such days. You may think I am hard to please – grumbling about four-pound chub. But I'm not really; I am always happy to catch chub like this, but on both occasions Ian and I were very unlucky. Just those few extra ounces would have turned two good days into two exceptional ones, for we fished hard and deserved every fish. I have since caught far larger chub for far less effort.

Besides chub, this reach also held some very good perch, and the Taylors were past masters at catching them. At that time I had never caught a two-pounder and was anxious to do so. 'Come with us – you'll catch one,' Fred said. So I went – and caught one!

The best conditions, Fred told me, were overcast, drizzly mornings. We arranged to meet one morning at dawn, and to my delight I awoke to find it drizzling. 'I'm putting you in 'No. 6' swim,' Fred told me on arrival, 'it's full of bulrushes but that's where they are.' (The reach in question was a match water, with permanent pegs in the bank – hence No. 6.) On Fred's instructions I tackled up with a float and 5-lb. b.s. line with a No. 6 hook tied direct. Now came the important bit. As perch spend most of their time in hiding, the plan was to cast upstream of a bulrush bed, and to allow the worm to trundle downstream as close to the stems as possible. This business of the worm rubbing the rush stems was, according to Fred, highly important.

For over two hours I trotted a lob past the bulrushes without success. Fred by this time had given it up as hopeless, for in this particular swim one did not normally have to wait long for a bite. Did the fault lie with the bait? In clear water brandlings were favourite, in coloured water, lobs. On this particular day the water was coloured. I tried brandling – no response – and soon reverted back to a lob.

Three hours passed, then four; still no bites. Suddenly the float stopped halfway along the rushes. It bobbed twice, then slid under, travelling upstream as it did so. I tightened gently and a good fish turned towards the rushes. Two-and-a-quarter pounds he weighed, and I don't know who was more pleased, Fred or I. 'You earned that fish,' Fred told me, and with all due modesty I had to agree.

In 1966 a tragedy occurred at Beachampton; the dredger reared its ugly head – or should I say bucket. Within a week what was once a meandering river with shallows, holes and rush beds, was turned into a shallow, featureless 'canal'. The chub and perch disappeared and, at the time of writing, have only just put in a reappearance.

Still, my visits to the Upper Ouse were not over. In 1968 I joined a syndicate who rented a reach a few miles upstream of Beachampton. It was full of roach – big roach – and with roach fishing at a premium I was naturally excited. And not without reason: what a season (or rather a winter) Fred Towns and I spent there!

The first roach I caught weighed about half-a-pound which, as it turned out, was a small one, for I only ever caught three roach *under* a pound. It was wonderful fishing, some of the best I have ever encountered.

The locals caught lots of roach, including some very large

bags indeed, and I was naturally interested in their tactics. Maggots were the popular bait, the method, trotting. But after two outings fishing that way I thought that better roach might be caught by other methods and baits. I have always said that, on most waters, bread fished stationary on the bottom will take the better roach. On my next visit I legered with breadcrust and straight away the quality increased. That day I met one of the locals who fished the water most weekends, but had not taken a roach over 1 lb. 7 oz. 'I just can't catch a one-and-a-half-pounder,' he told me, 'what do you suggest?' So I suggested. 'Forget maggots,' I told him, 'and try bread.' The next weekend he copped one 1 lb. 9 oz.

From then on, using bread, all the roach I caught topped the pound. Fred Towns also clobbered 'em, and we really enjoyed ourselves. But we were faced with a problem: that of hitting the bites. In my experience trying to hook roach at short range on leger tackle is a frustrating business. And during those first few weeks I was a very frustrated fisherman.

Of course I could have used a float – in fact I often did – when the problem does not arise. But it wasn't always possible to float-fish, and on those days I missed dozens of good bites. Eventually I reduced the missed bites to a minimum, and was finally hooking roach on the leger far more consistently than ever before.

The answer was a 'quiver tip'. Now I have never gone along with the notion that indicators are necessary in legering; I have always said, and always will, that *nothing* is so sensitive as one's finger. But sensitivity wasn't my problem; I could see the bites; the trouble was hooking them, and the rod top was to blame. The roach would pull at the bait then, feeling the rod top, drop it. The rod would bend, you struck – and missed.

One day Fred tried a swing-tip. His ratio of hooked fish increased immediately and Fred was fairly happy. I wasn't. A swing-tip has disadvantages (which I will not discuss here), and I wanted something that resembled a rod top. I decided to try a quiver tip.

The next day I bought a solid glass rod top and made one –

and didn't like the job one little bit; my, how those small glass fibres make one itch! But I was pleased with my results, and the following Saturday I settled down in a swim in which I was confident of getting bites. Bites came quickly, bites which, in contrast to those on the rod top proper, were decisive, starting with little pulls which gradually got longer until the quiver-tip was bent right over. That day I caught six good roach – an improvement on previous visits. But I still missed too many bites, and without any doubt the rod top was responsible.

If the roach pulled the quiver-tip decisively after the preliminary pulls and tugs it was possible to hook them – providing that they had mouthed the bait properly before the tip was pulled over to its limit. Most times, however, what happened was that the tip was pulled right over, finally pulling on the rod top proper. When this occurred the bite was missed, due no doubt to resistance. Although I had tapered the quiver-tip to offset this it obviously wasn't right. I had to think again.

Throughout the following weeks I made quiver-tips of different lengths and tapers, all of which, for various reasons, proved unsatisfactory. Some were too stiff, resulting in the roach giving sharp 'digs' and nothing more; others were too flimsy, snapping when an overhead cast was made. I began to despair; yet I had to find an answer.

Not that my quiver-tips were entirely unsatisfactory. Blank days were rare, and all the roach caught were good ones. But still too many bites were missed or failed to 'develop'. In the meantime, Fred was doing well with his swing tip, except when the water was really fast; then he started missing bites too.

What I wanted was a tip which the roach could pull without feeling resistance; one which would bend halfway then, as the pulls become stronger, would bend in the lower half but not on the rod top. It was apparent that the length and taper were vitally important.

The following weekend Fred showed me a quiver tip he had bought. It was much longer than those I had been making – 15 in., with an even diameter. I studied it closely. Would the extra length be an advantage? It might, but that taper – or lack of it? In my view this would present difficulties.

In practice this was proved correct (I used the tip before Fred had a chance!). Even with a moderate flow (one swan shot and one A.A. held bottom) the tip, because of its even diameter, bent over much too far. The roach had only to pull it an inch or two for it to tighten on the rod top. As soon as this occurred the bait was dropped.

Yet I liked the extra length. The following week I bought another tip (all my glass fibre had been used up) and began further experiments. I sliced an old quiver tip in half (that wasn't easy) then bound it on the bottom half of the new tip. With the base stiffened but with the top 7 in. unaffected I thought I was getting somewhere. I attached it to my rod top, threaded some line through and applied gentle pressure. Yes, this definitely looked better.

The day for testing coincided with our final trip of the season. The first bite came almost immediately. There were the familiar preliminary pulls, each one stronger than the last, and then a much better pull with only the top half of the tip moving. With hands at the ready I waited for the final decisive pull. It never came. And so the first hour's fishing proved fruitless.

This I couldn't understand. I was convinced that the roach could not feel resistance, for the tip was working beautifully. Eventually I struck at a bite and the tip snapped at the bottom where my splicing finished – a weak point I had overlooked. Despair! I hadn't another tip and the day was still young. The roach were obviously feeding so I reverted to a swing tip. And that, although I didn't know it then, was to convince me that the broken quiver tip was as near to perfection as I was likely to get.

The day was bitterly cold. The swing tip lifted an inch then a little higher, finally dropping back. It lifted again then, when halfway up, dropped again. Throughout the day these bites persisted, but I couldn't hit them. If I left it alone the bait was rejected. Little wonder the bites on the quiver-tip didn't develop, for the roach were in a finicky mood – the swing tip proved that. Fred, too, had proved many times that a swing-tip, in certain conditions, was superior to a quiver tip.

Weeks of experiment made it apparent that a quiver-tip with an even diameter was not very effective unless the water was dead slack, since the base bends far too early, creating resistance at the rod top. Neither will an ordinary length of glass serve – at least not where shy-biting fish are concerned, or where the current pull is above moderate. But my spliced model – ah, that was different, for it had gone a long, long way to solving an old problem. I could hardly wait for the new season to come round – by which time I would have some real 'quivers' properly made – and tapered.

For a moment I will bypass the events which took place that spring. Winter came, and one day I went chubbing on the Cherwell. The day was cold but the chub were biting – if you could call minute pecks and plucks, bites. Yet they were typical of cold-water chub bites, which most times do not develop, or if they do, take upwards of five minutes to do so. Would my 'quiver' bring results?; I decided to give it a try. The pecks turned into pulls! Since then, using a quiver, cold-water chub have proved far less troublesome and difficult to hit, for they can pull at the bait without feeling much resistance.

I have always said, and always will, that *nothing* is so sensitive as one's fingers, and that touch legering will beat all the indicators you care to mention. But I accept that there are exceptions, and my tapered quiver-tip has solved one roach problem and made one aspect of chub fishing more easy and enjoyable.

But back to the spring of that year. In May a tragedy struck: in less than a week over 900 big roach were wiped out by a mysterious pollution. Several months later Fred and I paid our old haunts a visit – and we never had a bite.

The Upper Ouse has been both kind and cruel to me. Firstly the dredging on Dick's reach – legal vandalism I called it – which ruined one of the finest fisheries it has been my privilege to fish; then the roach disaster. But that one season taught me a lot, for which I suppose I should be grateful.

7. *Opportunism: my first five-pound chub*

When the idea of this book first came to me I naturally cast my mind back to some of my most interesting catches. Whilst I was doing so it became very apparent that many of my best fish resulted from opportunities presented, and which I had quickly noted and taken full advantage of – opportunism, if you like. An important factor in angling this – highly important – much more so than anglers realise.

It is appropriate then, I suppose, that my first five-pound chub was taken in this manner. Not that it was a 'lucky' fish, no, I fished hard for it; nevertheless, it was a typical example of opportunism. In the previous chapter I have related how, on two occasions, I fished the Upper Ouse with a five-pounder in mind, but failed, despite the fact there were plenty in the water. I was to finally achieve my ambition in a water where five-pound chub are not common – the Thames. Not only that, the circumstances surrounding its capture were unusual and, therefore, worth relating.

A friend approached me one day to tell me about a reach of the Thames which, I must admit, I had never considered fishing. The particular stretch of water ran alongside a towpath and was very heavily fished, for it ran close to a busy main road. Reports, my friend said, had come in of big chub lying under the willows which lined the far bank. It was then summer, but I kept it in mind. Several months later, one January evening, a friend and I debated where we should fish on the morrow, and this reach came to mind. We decided to try it the following morning.

I awoke to find a heavy overnight frost – and that's an under-

OPPORTUNISM: MY FIRST FIVE-POUND CHUB

statement! We arrived at the waterside to find it deserted, which, considering the conditions, was not surprising. It was bitterly cold, the frost lying like snow on the banks and trees. I settled for a swim opposite one of the willows which looked particularly 'chubby', tackled up and settled down.

For three hours I fished hard without a sign of a bite. Because of the conditions I was using a small piece of crust on a No. 8 hook, with the lead stopped two inches away. There was no wind, and, although I never took my eyes off the rod top, it never moved. Even so, I liked the look of the water; it was, I thought, merely a matter of time before I had one.

After a while I decided to move a few yards downstream, and was just on the point of doing so when something happened that was to make all the difference. Suddenly, due to change in air temperature, the frost on the willows started to melt; it melted so quickly, however, that the smattering of the water surface under the trees could easily have been mistaken for heavy rain.

My first bite coincided with the heavy dripping from the trees. The rod top moved forward slowly about an inch, and a heavy fish bored along the far bank in response to my strike. A lively fight ensued before I had him in the net, one of the most beautifully conditioned chub I have ever seen. 'Well over four pounds,' I said to myself, and popped him into the keepnet.

The piece of crust had hardly settled on the bottom when the rod top moved again. This too, was a very small pull, but I do not reckon to miss these bites – and I didn't. Again, the rod bent right over and stayed whilst another chub resisted my attempts to pull him over. Eventually, however, he was beaten, this one even larger than the first, again in wonderful condition. It's not often in a season – especially in the Thames – when one catches two four-pound-plus chub in two casts, but this fish was well over that weight. With, I admit, trembling hands I cast again, the bait landing almost against the far bank under the trailing branches of the willows.

Very slowly the rod top pulled round an inch – no more.

This, too, was a good fish, certainly a four-pounder – three in as many casts, this really was something. I gave him plenty of 'stick' to get him away from the snaggy undergrowth, but once in midstream I relaxed the pressure a little. When I saw the broad back and large head I became excited, for this was an exceptional fish. Without much ado I coaxed him over the landing net and seconds later removed the hook from another good chub. I took a good look at its girth – a short thick fish this one, somewhat like those in the Ouse – and I decided to weigh it immediately. I could hardly believe my eyes when the balance pulled down to 5 lb. 1 oz. – my first five-pounder.

Something had happened since my last cast, however. I looked at the trees opposite; the water beneath them was now silent; the frost was no longer dripping from the overhanging branches. Somehow the water was different; the atmosphere of the previous ten minutes had gone. I flicked another piece of crust into the hole under the tree. This time, however, the rod tip didn't move; it still hadn't moved an hour later and for the remainder of the afternoon I didn't see another bite.

I carefully weighed the three fish before returning them to the water. As I said, three good ones; 5 lb. 1 oz.; 4¾ lb.; and 4¼ lb.

It was a remarkable ten minutes fishing. And whether it was coincidence or not I do not know, but the three bites all came during the period when the frost melted and dripped from the trees. If ever there was a case of opportunism, this was it.

What effect the melting frost would have upon the fish I hesitate to say – if it had any at all, of course. But it was a remarkable experience, one I have not encountered before or since. It was, and still is, the only time I have taken three-four-pound-plus chub in three casts. I returned home well satisfied.

Naturally the capture of those chub interested me, and for several weekends following I fished there again, taking a fair number of chub – all good ones – with a sprinkling of four-pounders. The reach, without doubt, held some very good chub and I awaited the following winter with great expectation. I was confident I could get to grips with them again.

OPPORTUNISM: MY FIRST FIVE-POUND CHUB

But it was not to be. The following winter came; I waited for the right conditions – water normal with the stream moderate to enable me to hold the tackle across the far bank – and went there again. A great shock greeted me. River officials, in an attempt to 'improve' the river, had decided the trees must go; no branches, just the stumps showing from the bank, which had a horrible 'bareness' about it. I fished, however, and for many days after, but without so much as a bite. I have not fished there since. It will be many, many years hence before the heavy frosts drip from those branches again.

A few weeks following this incident the level of the Thames dropped even lower, and my thoughts turned to a Thames weir-pool not far from my home. The pool is a big one, quite seventy yards across, and it can be fished from several different positions. Several years earlier I had plumbed one area thoroughly, for in this area I was catching a lot of fish. The plummet revealed a ledge running across the direction of the current and about twenty-five yards out from the bank. The ledge, as far as I could make out, was fairly high, but that isn't so important. What *is* important is that by placing a bait behind the ledge and close to it, more bites resulted. Accurate casting is vital if you wish to make the best of the swim.

Another point was that it fished best in winter, but conditions had to be just right; i.e. little current and low water. Now conditions were perfect, and one Friday I decided to snatch a couple of hours after work. I was home just after 4.30 p.m., grabbed my tackle, and cycled frantically down to the river.

I arrived to find just one gate open, the water racing along the far bank for a hundred yards, then back towards the weir again. At the point where it turned was the ledge, the eddying of the water being such that I could hold bottom almost against the ledge with three swan shots. As I said, ideal conditions.

At this point perhaps I had better say that the previous year, on the final weekend, I had found the pool in similar condition. That evening, in an hour, I took twelve chub weighing over 30 lb., with fish to 4¼ lb. Was this particular evening going to see a repetition of that visit?

Before tackling up I groundbaited heavily, the groundbait coming to rest somewhere close to the ledge. Having done this I tackled up with three swan shots on a sliding link, with a No. 6 hook attached. On this I placed a large piece of crust. With an overhead cast I placed my bait well past the ledge, allowed it to sink on a slack line, then, with the bait where I wanted it and the sun already set, I settled down.

Twenty minutes later I had a bite and caught him, a small fish of two pounds. I quickly made another cast; a cast that was to be the beginning of a wonderful, but strange, bit of fishing.

Now, as every leger angler knows, after the lead has reached bottom, you have to wait for the line to sink and tighten, and with a long cast in deep water this can take up to a minute. On the second cast, before the line had tightened the rod top pulled over about six inches, I struck, and not surprisingly, missed, for I had several feet of slack line to take up before hitting the fish. The same thing occurred on the next cast, and the next, and the next.

By this time I was getting desperate. There were not the usual inch and two-inch pulls which I am accustomed to, but pulls of up to eighteen inches or more. The bait was being taken immediately it hit bottom, and although the bites were bold enough to move the rod, it was – due to the line not being taut to the rod top – impossible to hook them.

All this time I groundbaited heavily, for I was most anxious to keep them in the swim whilst I tried to think of something. By now half an hour had passed; it was getting dark, and for all my exertions I had only two chub. If only they would leave the bait alone for a minute, then I would have them. And then, quite suddenly, they did.

I did not have long to wait. Immediately the line had tightened to the rod top, that familiar, slow confident bite came. But this was easy. That bite resulted in a four-pounder; the next cast – one slightly smaller. How many, I thought, could I get before dark?

I had taken six good chub when the resulting bite met with

OPPORTUNISM: MY FIRST FIVE-POUND CHUB

very solid resistance and the fish bored heavily way out against the ledge. I guessed it was an exceptional Thames chub, and I was quickly proved right – 5 lb. 2 oz. By now my groundbait supply had run out – I had used half a bucketful – and without this the bites decreased rapidly. Before it got too dark to see I took three more, making ten fish weighing 27 lb. Apart from the big chap two more topped four pounds, with a few slightly smaller.

As you can guess I enjoyed that hour in the weirpool, for apart from the actual catch it posed an interesting question: what to do when bites occur at long range so quickly that you haven't time to tighten the lead. That evening a huge bag was within my grasp, but initially it was impossible to hit the bites. Peter Drennan, who has had similar experiences with roach, suggests the use of a 14-ft. rod held high so that as little line as possible is in the water. He may be right, of course, and, although I have adopted such tactics with bream, the question still arises how to hook the fish successfully, for you can only bring the rod back two or three feet. Such a strike is sufficient at short range, but not over distances of thirty yards and more. Float fishing, for several reasons, is out of the question.

Overcasting, then pulling the bait and lead back into position may be the answer; due to the snaggy bottom, however, it was impossible in this particular swim. But in swims reasonably free of snags, this might well pay off.

It was dark when I packed. The bag was photographed and, apart from the five-pounder, carefully returned; the latter I retained in my outsize keepnet, for being alone I could not get the photographs I wanted. These I got next morning at daybreak, when, along with Ted Robbins, I returned, hoping to contact the shoal again.

We tackled up in pouring rain; rain that was to continue all day. For ten hours we fished that swim, always hoping that the magic might return, but it didn't. We never had a fish.

8. Days amongst the bream

It was a warm, sunny July evening: the date 1947. Fred Smith and I were fishing a Thames backwater when suddenly Fred hooked a fish which appeared somewhat heavier than the normal-sized chub we were catching. 'Dunno what this is,' Fred remarked, 'it's big and bronzy.' Suddenly the fish broke surface; 'Crikey,' I said, 'it's a bream – fancy that!' Four-and-a-half pounds it weighed – I took it home and cooked it! It was the first bream I had ever seen – and the last I ever ate!

One close, humid morning two months later, two hundred yards downstream of Moulsford Bridge on the Thames, I caught my first-ever bream – in fact, I caught two, both at once, for I was using two hooks; a common practice in those days. That day a bream-fisher was born.

Until then, bream were scarce in the Upper Thames. In March 1947 we experienced one of the worst floods on record (we lived upstairs for several days), and from then on bream appeared in considerable numbers. Where they came from – if indeed they came from anywhere – is anybody's guess – but come they did, and how. Within a year vast shoals had congregated in some reaches, and several large bags were taken. By 'large' I mean twenty and thirty pounds, with an average weight of two pounds or so. I became interested – very! – and quickly caught 'bream-fever', a disease which was destined to remain with me for many years. For it wasn't just catching bream that interested me; they presented problems – big problems.

I dreamt of bream, not just big ones but an outsize bag – 100 lb. or so. This target I knew would not be easy to attain, for so many factors were involved. There was the problem of location; the business of holding the shoal long enough to make

Ted Robbins weighs his big barbel – 10½ lb.

... I had never seen a 'cat' before, and believe me it isn't a pleasant sight

Bringing a 30 lb. tope to the side

The author and tope

ABOVE: The author returns a nice Blenheim pike. BELOW LEFT: A 17 lb. pike finally beaten. BELOW RIGHT: Fred Towns, and pike 27½ and 17 lb., taken on wobbled deadbait at Blenheim

ABOVE: The author and a 5 lb. 2 oz. Thames chub. BELOW: A 27 lb. catch of Thames chub taken by the author from one swim. Best fish 4 lb. 6 oz.

130 lb. of bream, on the occasion when the author packed with the fish still biting

Unhooking a Test trout taken on a fly

ABOVE: Tough characters, these gravel-pit tench. BELOW: Bringing an Annan chub ashore. They came so thick and fast that no net was used!

'The third weekend ... I actually walked along the Thames into Oxford!'

A roach which tipped the scales at 2¼ lb.

a haul, plus the problem of sorting out the larger members of the shoal.

Where location was concerned I found it best to look for bream rolling, then fish in that area. On the Upper Thames they rolled in three different ways, and the manner in which they did so taught me whether I was in with a chance or not. If they 'head and tailed' the shoal was moving and impossible to hold; if they flapped the surface with their tails as they went down our chances were fair. But if the rolling took the form of swirls then nine times out of ten the fish intended remaining in that area.

But if they didn't roll – what then? In those days three or four of us usually fished together and, working on the assumption they must be feeding somewhere, I devised a plan.

Placing ourselves about ten yards apart we would fish for about ten minutes. One of the end men would then move along the line down past the others and place himself ten yards below the other end man. Five minutes later the man who was originally next to him would do the same, and so on. I called it my 'cross-over' method, and on days when the bream were not showing it often led us to a shoal.

I didn't always leger, and one day when 'trotting' I discovered that if I lowered the float a few inches I caught bigger fish. Shortly after, a friend called round to say that he had seen a massive shoal on the Cherwell, in which the fish were lying in layers, the medium-sized ones well down, the better fish on top, with a few outsize fish almost on the surface. From then on, 'bream layers' became an important factor.

As my knowledge of bream increased so did my catches, and on several occasions I topped forty pounds. Then, in July 1959, it happened: I caught a big bag.

All was quiet and still as I made my way up river. Dawn had not long broken, and to reach my destination I had started early. In those days I was a keen match angler, and on this particular Sunday my club were fishing a match. I eventually reached the meeting point, sweating under my load, for I was not travelling light. Apart from tackle, two big canvas buckets were full with groundbait, which, in order to lessen the load, was dry.

Since my interest in bream was aroused I had never gone unprepared in respect of groundbait. Many, many times I had been tempted to leave the bulk, weighing some half-hundredweight, behind, but, forever aware of its importance, it was always taken and – much to my sorrow – brought home again.

One by one the competitors arrived, and much speculation took place as to the prospects. At 7.30 a.m., with everyone assembled, the draw for pegs took place. I forget what my number was now, but that does not matter. A short walk found me at my pitch, where a small hawthorn bush hung over the bank. Little did I know it then, but that bush was later to become the most famous landmark along the entire fishery.

The bank at this point was straight for two hundred yards, turning into a deep eddy further downstream. On my bank no marginal rushes existed, no stream was running, and the water was slightly coloured. In fact it looked uninteresting, and I honestly believed that I should do well to catch a few roach.

Float or leger, which should it be? I decided upon the former and, within a few minutes, was tackled up. Another five minutes saw the groundbait mixed and, with a little time to go before the whistle, I sat down and waited.

The morning was still, close, and humid, with a slight west wind blowing from my back. The voices of far-off anglers could be heard and I was listening to their conflicting opinions, slightly drowsy from the early rising, when the whistle sounded. Having a vague idea only as to the bottom contours of my swim the first few minutes were spent with the plummet. This revealed a contrasting bottom indeed; twelve feet of water under my bank gradually sloping off to five feet within two yards of the opposite bank. Nothing very exciting in fact, so I elected to fish mid-river in nine feet of water.

The first hour and a half produced two small gudgeon. Nothing I tried would entice a roach, yet the roach fishing in this reach was very good indeed.

There was something mysterious about it all. The morning had remained dark for the time of day. Everyone as far as I could see was fishless, and only constant casting and occasional laughter could be heard. Then suddenly, quite suddenly, someone caught a fish, a bream of some three pounds, quickly followed by another. Then his neighbour caught one of similar size, this continuing down the line until the competitor next to me was also bending into a bream. But I, despite frequent changing of baits and trying various depths, remained fishless – in fact biteless.

I was, I admit, bewildered. That bream were in the vicinity of my swim there was little doubt, so, standing up, I took a look around. My eyes searched the river from left to right then suddenly focused upon two water lilies near the far bank. I wondered; was there a patch of underwater lilies ('cabbages') in front of me? If so, that would be where I would expect a shoal to feed.

Hastily dismantling my tackle I fixed up my leger rod, a 3-lb. b.s. line, with a single swan shot on a 'sliding link'. Pinching a piece of paste on the hook I cast to within three yards of the far bank, where I hoped it would settle amongst the lilies.

My line was now lying on the surface. A few seconds later it sank, my eyes focused on the rod top. Did I perceive a movement? I was not sure, but I struck. Something heavy and immovable was on the end of the line, and, amid great excitement, I increased pressure. A section of a lily leaf floated to the surface (so there was a 'cabbage patch' out there); furthermore, big bream which I had for so long sought, but never found. Slowly, very slowly, the fish – now out of the 'cabbages' – made its way upstream, boring and thumping on the rod top, the line singing in the wind. How that bream fought, so different from those found in still-waters, but I was winning and suddenly saw a bronze flash a few yards from the bank. But it wasn't finished yet; several times the clutch screamed as the fish turned away, before it slid over my big net. A fair fish I thought as I placed him into the keepnet – 5 lb. perhaps. Now

I really had to work to keep the shoal interested.

Kneading half a bucket of groundbait into hard balls, I threw these across to the far bank, and put another large dose to soak, picked up the rod, re-baited and cast, again into the 'cabbage patch'. Due to the light lead the line took a full minute to sink and tighten, but immediately it did so I again detected a slight movement on the rod top. I struck and met with solid resistance. 'Pumping' quickly shifted it from the cabbages, but it wasn't giving up easily. It was, I should think, a full three minutes before I was able to sink the landing net and three minutes is a long time to play a fish. This fish too was a good one – identical in size to the first one – and quickly joined its companion in the keepnet.

Attention was once more called to the groundbait. Another half a bucketful was thrown in, more mixed, and a few minutes later a third bream was landed, then another, and another, until the number had risen to ten. A problem then arose – the keepnet. Mine was a respectable size, but could not take many more. Every bream was over 4 lb., and I began to think in terms of a heavy bag.

But a second – more serious – problem had arisen. The groundbait supply had now dwindled to nothing, and, without any, the shoal would surely move on. By this time, however, my fellow competitors had become interested in the proceedings and many, having packed their gear, were sat watching me. One, bless him, brought along his large supply of groundbait – a very sporting action and one which was greatly appreciated.

I again groundbaited heavily, and checking on the time discovered that little more than one and a half hours remained before the whistle. I decided to go all out for a 100-lb. bag, but I had to move fast. I reckoned that quite half a minute elapsed from the time my bait hit the water to the moment when the line tightened to the rod top, so I added a second shot to speed up the operation. I tightened up quicker all right. But not a bite materialised and it was obvious that on this particular occasion the bait had to sink slowly to interest the bream. I quickly removed the second shot, and upon the line tightening was into another fish. This one, like the others, fought like fury, not just the slow determined 'thump' so typical of bream, but actual runs which forced me to give line. I have caught hundreds of barbel, and weight for weight no barbel ever fought better than those bream.

By this time odd fish were swirling on the surface right over the 'cabbage patch' but at no time did one actually show itself – in my experience a rare occurrence. As each fish was hooked a lily leaf would break off and I lost several bream that just would not be bullied out. Still I plodded on; my keepnet would not take any more – at least with comfort. But another was soon produced from somewhere and I looked again at my watch – half an hour to go.

All this time the onlookers had crept closer and closer in an effort to detect the bites, but in vain. Not once, they assured me did they see one, and I must admit the bites were most feeble, yet at the same time confident, ones. I tried watching the line, but the breeze prevented bite detection. All the fish were hooked by watching the rod top, and not once did it move further than half an inch.

I was playing the last fish as the whistle sounded, and upon landing it made a great mistake – I packed. What made me do this I just cannot think, but I did with the bream still biting freely. In retrospect I may not have caught many more for the second supply of groundbait had also vanished. Nevertheless, it was a bad mistake.

Now came the business of weighing my bag. In two and a half hours I had taken twenty-three fish, two were about a pound each, but the remaining 21 scaled $86\frac{1}{4}$ lb., best fish $5\frac{1}{2}$ lb., all except one returned safely to the water.

A fortnight later Ted Robbins, Pete Drennan, a lad called Seamus and I went there again. No bream rolled and none were caught. About 8 a.m. we put my 'cross-over' plan into operation, and eventually located the shoal a hundred yards upstream of the bush. I started off by catching fish in the four-to-five-pound bracket, but the others could only catch small ones between two and three pounds. We were fishing 'tight', so tight that our lines were crossed and tangles were frequent. 'Watch it, Drennan, you're over me,' one would say, 'Then pull up,' would come back the reply, 'I've got to fish, ain't I!' Sometimes one would strike to find himself into a fish – but not on *his* hook. It was an hilarious morning.

By 11 a.m. we had a fair bag, but our groundbait supply had dwindled. We had come by pushbike, and between us and home were three miles of very bumpy fields. But who cared – certainly not I – and I was soon away pedalling furiously, my backside rarely, if ever, touching the saddle. I returned 'all in' (ever tried pushbiking with 40 lb. of groundbait swaying on the handlebars?) to find the bream still going. And – strange this – whoever had sat on my stool, no matter where he cast, had caught the big fish – no one else. The fresh supply kept them going for a further two hours then it was all over. 130 lb. the bag weighed, best fish almost 6 lb.

During the next five years I fished for bream week in week out. I can't remember all the bags my friends and I caught, but man, it was plenty! One afternoon, in blazing sunshine, Fred Smith and I took 88 lb. of fish between four and five and a half pounds. I took mine trotting well out with brandlings (what a fine bream bait they are). Sometimes the float would slowly sink; sometimes it travelled upstream; sometimes downstream travelling faster and faster as it did so, or go crash-bang-under – just like that! What it *didn't* do was tilt over then glide slowly out of sight – as most of the text books say it does.

Other catches which spring to mind are 130 lb. I took alone on float-fished bread and which could have been more. But despite fishing at different depths I could *not* stop catching two- and three-pounders, so I eventually packed with the fish still biting. Another 130 lb. with Fred J. Taylor in a weirpool (one of many large bags from that pool); ten fish weighing 52 lb. taken in half an hour; I could go on...

One big bag I shall always remember fell to Fred Towns and I one afternoon in 1969. It was one of those days when everything clicked; conditions were good, the sun shone and the fish remained in one spot for hours. Yet despite our large bag we should have caught more – many more. Why? Well, let's start from the beginning.

I had just finished lunch and was about to take the family out for the afternoon when the phone rang. John Everard was on the other end. 'Fred has got the bream going,' John said, 'you know where he is.' Within minutes I had changed back into old clothes whilst my long-suffering wife, Sue, cut some sandwiches knowing that her afternoon out was cancelled. I gathered my tackle, loaded 40 lb. of groundbait into a canvas bucket and was gone.

I drove the twelve miles cursing under my breath. I had promised to meet Fred at dawn but when the alarm woke me at 4 a.m. it was bucketing down with rain. I hate fishing in rain, even more so starting out in it, so I had stayed indoors thinking Fred would do likewise. Apparently he hadn't, and now the weather had changed for the better with the sun beating down from a cloudless sky.

I parked the car and began the mile-long walk to the river, my tackle and groundbait loaded on a trolley. I say 'walk', actually I ran for I was anxious to reach Fred before the shoal departed – if they hadn't already done so. Twenty minutes later, amid much puffing and panting I saw Fred in the distance. 'How many?' I enquired when I eventually reached him. 'About seventy pounds,' he replied, 'but they have gone off – I've run out of groundbait.' It didn't take me long to mix some more which we tossed into the swim in large handfuls. Before I could tackle up Fred's rod was bending again – the groundbait was working. The river, Fred said, was getting progressively faster; whereas he had started off with one swan shot on a link he was now using two. He was legering with pieces of breadcrust on a No. 10 hook, the line 6-lb. b.s.

I sat immediately below Fred and was into fish right away – fish between three and four pounds. The bites were gentle, the rod top pulling over about an inch – often less than that. Some anglers say that bream are easy, but that's not strictly true. I have caught big bags when the rod has been pulled right round, it's true, but I've taken far more when the bites have been small, insignificant affairs. Remember that 84-lb. bag mentioned earlier when the gallery of spectators swore they never saw a bite? But I am digressing...

For over three hours we clobbered the bream and it became hard work (who said fishing was relaxing?). If I wasn't landing fish I was mixing groundbait. Not that it holds the shoal in the true sense of the word – it would take more like 400 lb. than 40 to hold a bream shoal – but it does concentrate them into a confined area long enough for one to make a haul.

By tea-time we had four large keepnets in operation and they were still biting. One thing bothered me however; although few fish were under two pounds, none topped five and it was the big fish we wanted. The question of 'bream layers' kept going through my mind; were the larger fish either at the top, underneath or in the middle? We were using crust with our leads stopped 12 inches from the hook, so the bait was roughly that distance off bottom. 'Perhaps the bigger chaps are lower down Fred,' I said, 'let's see.'

I replaced the crust with flake. The lead touched bottom and the rod top pulled round slightly. I struck and a heavy fish bored in the current. Five and a quarter pounds! A minute later I copped another – 5 lb. 1 oz. Fred, in the meantime, stayed with crust and caught two more three-pounders.

By this time the river was flowing strongly and I was using a ¾ oz. weight; at this rate fishing would soon be impossible, so we decided to pack. 'Just one more cast,' I said, and casting out another piece of flake I stood up. I *thought* I saw the rod top move but wasn't sure, but I bent down and struck. As I did so, a fish tore off down stream with the clutch screaming.

My, how that fish fought. Those who say bream can't fight should have seen that one go. For over three minutes I played him, by which time two passing launches had stopped opposite to watch. Suddenly a big dorsal fin broke surface – with my hook protruding from it. 'Foul-hooked,' I said, 'I'll get a better look, and if it's under five pounds I'll break off.' I coaxed the fish in further and it turned sideways. 'Don't know about five,' I said, 'it's nearer six.'

At that moment the fish turned towards midstream and with one almighty dash tore off across the river, its dorsal still showing. I've caught a few bream but that was the fastest I have ever known – it would have done a salmon credit! There was little I could do and I didn't stop him until it had almost reached the far bank. Now he was beaten and with much protesting I pulled him back over the waiting net. Six pounds ten ounces he weighed, and on that happy note we packed.

We weighed Fred's bag first – 130 lb. – then mine, a modest 76 lb. seventy fish with a total catch of 206 lb. – not a bad catch. I made one mistake; not trying flake sooner, for the three fish I caught on flake were the three biggest in the entire bag.

But the question still remains: what might our bag have been had I not 'chickened out' during the early hours when Fred really had them going? My decision to stay indoors probably cost us a record-breaking catch.

In latter years bream fishing on the Upper Thames has deteriorated somewhat, and these days I do very little. No longer are big bags caught with almost monotonous regularity, and 100-lb. bags – once common – are today almost unheard of. But if I never catch another bream I've had my share – and more. Someone asked me once what I consider my best ever bream catch – a difficult question, for there have been so many. But I *do* know: the 84 lb. I caught in that match. The memories of the two hundred pounds, and the many hundreds will never outshine those of that close, humid morning when I sat alongside that little hawthorn bush.

9. Trout on the fly

Mention the Cotswolds and the lovely meandering river Windrush springs to mind. Unless I'm seeking a big, old Thames trout, trout fishing to me means fly fishing, both wet and dry. I'm no purist – not even when fishing a fly – and a wet-fly fished downstream is, to me, as skilful – if not more so – as fishing a dry-fly.

I can't remember what year it was when I first cast a fly on the Windrush, but I remember the occasion quite clearly. A friend of mine, Alec Adamson, is not only a very fine coarse angler but he can cast a fly – and catch trout – with the best of them. So when Alec invited me to have a go at the Windrush trout I accepted without hesitation.

Although I had never fished wet-fly before it didn't take me long to get the hang of it. For wet-fly fishing is akin to legering; you simply cast upstream (that's important as you will see later) and across, then, as the fly comes towards the bank you watch the line and feel for the bites. Simple – at least I found it so.

It was the second week in April – the beginning of the wet-fly season. On this particular day Alec showed me the river, gave me some of his flies (and what fish-catchers they proved to be) and left me to it. Under a line of willows the water flowed deep and steady with shallows well out from my bank. It looked decidedly 'trouty', and I was soon tackled up. On the 'point' I tied an Invicta with, I think, a Partridge and Orange on the dropper. But that doesn't matter; what *does* matter is that my first cast landed upstream of the top tree with the line well sunk by the time it reached the trees. As the 'bow' in the line straightened I felt a long, heavy pull and tightened. After a good scrap I netted a 'takeable' trout. I shall always remember that fish, and the other five I took that afternoon, all on wet-fly fished deep.

It wasn't long before I became a member, and for several seasons I spent many happy hours catching trout in all sorts of weather. April and May were the best months, and when the wet-fly was most effective; once the weeds grew to the surface (and the Windrush gets very weedy indeed) it was dry fly only.

Over the years I got to know several of the members very well and one thing surprised me; very few could really master the wet-fly technique. This often led to arguments for and against the wet-fly. One day I had taken two nice trout and met up with a member who was a real purist. He asked how I had fared and how I had caught them. 'Oh like *that*,' he said, 'don't believe in the method, should be banned; a wet-fly upstream yes, but downstream – no.'

Honestly, such talk makes me furious, and I strongly suspect that the reason why many frown upon wet-fly downstream is they can't fish it effectively. Why can't they? I think I know the answer to that one too.

Most of those I watched fishing 'wet' would persist in casting across and downstream – just like the good books say you should. This is what happens. You cast, but by the time the fly sinks, the line is straight or nearly so. A trout takes and turns downstream, and one of two things happens: either the rod is whipped round violently, or the trout feels resistance and drops the fly. When the rod is whipped round it is very, very difficult indeed to hook the trout. And if it drops the fly, well ... you can't hook a fish that hasn't got the hook in its mouth, can you?

But by casting across and *upstream* a vastly different situation arises. The fly sinks, the bow in the line straightens, and the fly rises to the surface – like a hatching fly. The trout takes (they invariably do at this moment) swims off, and the line tightens, *but slowly*. You can't miss!

Alec's flies, I am sure, made a difference too. Not only does he tie a nice fly, but also he uses the right hackles – hackles from old birds with plenty of 'sheen' on them. I seldom used more than half a dozen patterns for I firmly believed the 'sheen' and correct presentation was sufficient. At least I found it so.

But I didn't always fish 'wet' – not by a long way. In my initial season I looked forward to the mayfly season – 'duffers fortnight' they call it. But not for me it wasn't. I caught trout, it's true, but I worked hard for every fish; in addition, every member seemed to be abroad when I was, but – and this bucked me up no end – no one else fared much better than me. Something was wrong, and I decided to see Dick Walker about it.

Dick didn't give me much advice; instead he gave me a dozen of his special 'Mays'. And what 'mays' they were – twice, almost three times, the size of a normal 'May'. All had different coloured hackles too; some green; some yellow, some winged, some not. One wingless pattern had orange and white hackles; a more unnatural looking mayfly I have yet to see.

One afternoon I watched an angler casting a 'May' over a rising fish. 'Rising' did I say? Actually the fish spent more time sucking in naturals than it spent looking at them. In other words it was going dotty. For almost an hour I watched the angler casting – and what a lovely caster he was – but without success. Several times a natural was taken inches from his fly and finally, not wishing to embarrass the poor chap too much, I continued my way upstream.

Three hours later I returned; the trout was still rising and the angler still casting. 'No good then?' I asked. 'No,' he replied, 'I'll give him best – you try.' On went one of Dick's creations; I cast, up came the trout and took it like a lamb! I can still see the look on the poor chap's face now. When I cleaned the trout it was so full of mayflies they were actually protruding from its throat.

Yes, Dick's 'mays' were real killers, and I caught many good trout on them. Or at least *some* of them. Those with the yellow hackles were far less successful than the green ones, and the most life-like pattern of the lot never raised a fish. I found the hackle patterns best, probably because I could never get the winged ones to land upright!

My 'best' trout was caught one hot afternoon in June. The 'mays' were up, and I spotted a good fish rising against my bank in two feet of water. I approached him carefully and placed my favourite pattern well upstream of him. Up he came, then, inches away, stopped short. I tried again; this time it didn't move. I tried a different pattern; the trout showed interest but hardly moved off the bottom. I placed a winged pattern over him and up he came to it like a rocket, opened his mouth then changed his mind. I tried the same fly again (it landed upright!) but no interest was shown.

This continued for almost half an hour; some patterns would interest the trout; others had no effect whatsoever. There was just one pattern left – the orange and white creation. I had nothing to lose, so on it went. The fly landed well upstream of the trout but before I could gather my wits it had gone – *never* have I seen a trout move so fast! He paid the penalty; a well-earned fish. But since then I have never caught, or even rose, another trout on that fly.

One day I decided to fish the lower beat. I had never fished there before and, after taking a few fish on the 'may', I came to what I thought was the boundary fence. Twenty yards below the fence were some shallows where several good trout were rising. I looked for a notice board but there wasn't one. And there was no angler in sight whom I could ask. Believing it must be club water I crossed the fence and in double quick time had two good trout. And there were more for the taking. But I had my limit, and after catching a third fish which I returned, gave it best.

The following spring I received an invitation from a farmer to fish his reach of the Windrush – a reach which was rarely, if ever, fished. After the usual introductions I made my way upstream and after a long walk came upon a swim in which a number of trout were rising. And the swim looked familiar – very much so. The horrible truth then dawned upon me: the previous year I had been poaching.

In the farmer's cottage that evening my host asked what I thought of his water. 'Very nice,' I said, 'especially right upstream; the trout appear to congregate in that area.' 'Ah yes,' he replied, 'twenty yards above the shallows is my boundary fence and the club above stock it every year, so they are never disturbed.' I didn't have the nerve to let on, and if he ever reads this, well John . . . I'm sorry!

Today I am no longer a member of the club, and I haven't cast a fly on the Windrush for years. And I miss it; the long, slow, pull on the line as the 'bow' straightens; or the trout rising to my outsize 'mays' are now just memories. Yes, I miss it very much indeed.

10. Creek mullet

'You must take a walk down to Mudeford Marsh and have a go at those mullet; the water is boiling with 'em – you'll catch a sackful. High tide is at three this afternoon, can you make it? You can? – good, be here at half past two.'

It was the first day of our holiday and Sue and I had just arrived at our 'digs' – the 'Dolphins' at Mudeford, run by Malcolm and Doreen Dore. Both are keen anglers, and Malc was telling me about the mullet. Never having caught one I was naturally interested, so . . . half past two it was.

Mudeford Marsh is a large expanse of marshy ground situated between the entrance to Christchurch harbour and Mudeford Quay. At high tide the water covers a large channel running parallel between the two quays, and it is up this channel the mullet come. And how they come; not dozens but hundreds, many of them big ones. As the 'flood' nears its 'top', the channel becomes a turmoil – and that's an understatement indeed – of wildly thrashing mullet, half-rolling, swirling and darting as far as the eye can see. I can only describe it as a fantastic sight, one worth going miles to see.

Upon arrival I tackled up with a roach rod, 3-lb. b.s. line, a small float and a No. 16 hook; the bait was maggots. Casting into the swirling mass I watched and waited; the maggots were ignored. Now hadn't I read somewhere that bread paste was a good mullet bait? – but that too was ignored. To cut a very long story short, I tried brandlings, rag, lug, live shrimps – all to no avail. I float-fished, legered, free-lined – the lot. But nothing.

So I stopped fishing and watched. On to the shallows charged half a dozen mullet chasing shrimps. On went another free-lined shrimp alive, which I retrieved in small jerks. Nothing.

'By God,' I said to myself, 'if these were chub I'd murder 'em on floating crust.' Floating crust – ah, that was an idea. I changed the hook for a No. 8, and on it placed a small piece of crust. A 'hump' appeared under the crust; then another – and one took it. I struck and missed – damn! Still, at least they liked crust, so on went another piece. Another 'hump' then a s...u...c...k and it was gone. I tightened, and shortly after landed my first ever mullet, a fish just over 2½ lb.

'Oh yes,' I thought, 'that's the stuff for these creek mullet; soon have another one.' What a laugh; – I didn't have another offer – not one. And now, four years later, the situation hasn't changed. Every year I'm there I try them, but I have never had another bite.

This puzzles me, and I'll tell you why. 'Round the corner' in the entrance to Christchurch harbour still more mullet abound and anglers catch them – without much bother either. Why then, should a 'catchable' fish become 'uncatchable' simply because it swims a few yards from a harbour entrance to a creek. It just doesn't make sense – only to the fish of course.

I recently read two articles on mullet. The first one – written by someone who lives in Mudeford – advised ragworm fished under a float, saying that by this method mullet are easy. Well, I respect his views although I certainly do not agree with them. And he was writing about creek mullet. The second writer was, I thought, much nearer the mark. He listed several different methods and baits (all successful in Christchurch harbour) and he ended by saying 'but creek mullet – ah, they are different, shy, difficult, almost impossible to catch.'

So...if my reader knows how to catch creek mullet, *please* let me know. Not only have I a score to settle, but I'm up the creek too!

11. Fishing for television

During the winter of 1966 I was invited by my good friend Jonathan Webb to make a five-minute film for B.B.C. Television. Although it wasn't the first time I had appeared on the 'box', it was the first time I had been given a completely free hand to choose a water and catch what I liked. I gladly accepted the offer.

In order to make the film as interesting as possible I opted for a small stream where, by crawling about on my stomach and fishing over barbed wire fences, I might catch a few chub. Filming was to take place on the Sunday, so this kept the Saturday free for me to give the water the once over.

One bank is club water, the other private. Permission had been obtained to fish from the private bank for it was essential that no other anglers should be trampling the bank whilst I was fishing. There would be enough disturbance from the camera crew and it was vital this was kept down to a minimum.

On the Saturday morning I fished the club bank. At one point a willow reaches out into the water on the opposite bank and it's a tricky swim to fish. The drill is to get well upstream of the tree, cast over with as little weight on the line as possible, allow the bait to trundle down until it is almost under the tree then walk quickly downstream three or four yards holding the rod high. You are then upstream legering with the bait right under the tree. All very tricky.

On the first cast the line fell slack – $3\frac{3}{4}$ lb. Ten minutes later it fell slack again – 3 lb. this one. This was encouraging for the morrow, and I moved upstream to another good swim. But my joy was shortlived. When, five hours later I packed, I hadn't had another bite; this on a water where I expect a lot. Clearly it wasn't going to be easy the following day.

Next morning, Jonathan and I arrived well before the cameramen. I decided to leave the 'tree swim' for later; in the meantime I would try a swim not fishable from the club bank. Here the water ran swiftly with a ledge a little way out. Due to barbed wire it could only be fished upstream and over the fence. A difficult swim, but decidedly 'chubby'.

Poking the rod through the fence I flicked a piece of crust upstream, allowed it to settle, then took up the slack. The lead rolled towards me, then the line dropped sharply. A long sweep back of the rod, a brief struggle, and out he came – $3\frac{1}{2}$ lb. I cast again. Once more the line fell slack – another three-pounder. The next cast produced a different bite – a big pull – unusual, I find, when upstream legering. I struck, only to clip a willow with the top joint. A swirl, and he was gone.

Next cast the line fell slack, but only slightly; I really couldn't tell whether it was a bite or not. But I was latched into a heavy fish. For a full minute it hung deep, never once showing, then suddenly the hook came adrift. I cursed; very rarely do I have chub come off and if it was a chub then it was a good 'un. But there are also barbel present...

Obviously this was a good swim, and we decided it would be the one for filming. I threw in some bread and moved out.

Soon after the cameras arrived, and, although the cameramen respected my wishes for quietness, the bankside disturbance was considerable. Whilst they were getting ready I groundbaited steadily – not to get the fish in the swim, of course, but to keep them interested. Eventually all was ready.

I crept down the bank, flicked my bait into the swim and prayed for the line to fall slack. Suddenly it did. 'Fish on,' I shouted, and the cameras started to roll. But it was no chub – a rotten two-pound bream. I unhooked it and cast again. But the chub had gone. For half an hour the line never moved. I was just debating what to do next when the problem was solved for me.

At this point the owner's son arrived to say that I could fish upstream of the fence in his garden. This water was completely new to me, but I knew it held a good head of fish. My heart was thumping as I crossed the lawn to the river.

The water is shallow with a small pool at one end. I would try the pool, and full of confidence instructed the crew to get ready. Whilst they were doing so I crossed the river and peered into the pool. It was crawling with chub.

I signalled to the camera crew, and flicked a piece of crust well downstream. Before I could collect my wits the rod pulled round – chub number one. I cast again. Once more the rod top pulled over and another chub came protesting to the net. The next cast produced another, then all went quiet.

'Just one more,' the director shouted – 'a nice one to finish with.'

In one corner of the pool was a little 'slack'; into this I cast a piece of crust. Ten minutes elapsed before the rod top flickered – just. But I saw it; I struck, and a minute later a $3\frac{1}{2}$-pounder was lifted from the water. Mission completed!

During the next two or three years I made several films both for B.B.C. and I.T.V., and was naturally pleased to catch fish on all of them. Catching fish with a camera crew buzzing around behind, sideways and in front of you isn't easy – especially shy fish like chub. Some of the jobs were difficult – one in particular. Funny thing was, I didn't know what was going on until I arrived at the water.

An east wind blew across the Avon as I stopped the car outside the old mill. It was February, my first visit to the water, and I was not hopeful. The east wind was bad enough; in addition the water was gin-clear. It would be hard fishing, just how hard I was soon to discover.

Tony Fordham had made arrangements by telephone, and the line had been faulty. Conversation had been difficult, but I thought I heard Jack Hargreaves mentioned. But Jack surely, would be busy filming.

But Jack wasn't – he was at the mill. Not only that, but he wanted to feature me on his 'Out Of Town' programme. By now Tony had arrived, and after the customary greetings we made our way inside out of the bitter wind.

'Now then Peter,' Jack said, 'what I require is this. I want you to leger and catch three fish: a big dace, a big roach and a chub. In addition, you must catch one by upstream legering, one downstream and the other across. I realise that conditions are right against fishing and if you don't fancy it say so. But I receive so many letters saying that angling writers can't fish I want to prove them wrong, so what about it?' Being game for anything, I consented, although I knew my task was a difficult one. Jack never did believe in making things easy.

I had never seen the water before so, in company with Jack, I made my way downstream, my first job to select a dace swim. Immediately below a hawthorn bush the water shallowed, the bottom plainly visible. This was what I was looking for – shallows below a deep run.

Dace are reputed to be fast biters, almost impossible to hook on the leger. In my experience, however, this isn't true – at least as far as big dace are concerned. It's simply a matter of getting the angle of the line right, other factors being equal of course.

A barbed wire fence (again!) ran parallel with the river, which meant I had to fish over the fence with the rod pointing skywards. On a 4-lb. b.s. line I placed a link leger with two swan shots attached, stopped four inches from a No. 10 hook; bait crust. I introduced a small handful of breadcrumbs then, resting the rod on the fence, held the line between my fingers, my eyes glued to the rod top.

The bitter wind blew the rod top to and fro, but I suddenly noticed a different movement. I struck and a dace of 6 oz. swirled on the surface. So the first of my three tasks was successfully completed; now for the second – a big roach.

Three hours later I still hadn't got the roach – or even had a bite for that matter. It was now two o'clock and my hands were very, very cold. The east wind blew even harder and I was worried. There was, however, one place which might produce a roach – the mill pool. There, in the fast water, they might feed.

I studied the pool carefully and decided to leger upstream in some turbulent water at the 'tail'. Crust again, but because I was legering upstream I removed one shot, leaving one. I cast well upstream of the swim; the shot held bottom, moving position slightly as I raised the rod. Just right.

My hands were perished but I held the rod; if a bite came I dare not miss it. A minute passed; suddenly the line fell slack. I struck, and a big roach swirled on the surface. Then the hook pulled free. In his commentary Jack said I was talking to myself: I was too, but will not say what I said.

Ten minutes later the line fell slack again; once more I felt a heavy fish throbbing in the current. I played it carefully and, with the camera ticking away, finally steered it over the net. $1\frac{1}{4}$ lb. – a good fish.

That was two; one more wanted – the chub. I decided my present position gave me the best chance, but the chub had to be caught legering across stream. I re-positioned myself and, with a slightly larger piece of crust, cast across into a small 'slack'.

A gentle pull on the line, almost missed by my numbed fingers. I felt the fish but it wasn't a chub. As I suspected, another roach four ounces smaller than the first. Normally, such a fish would please me, but it was a chub I wanted now – nothing else.

It was now well past four o'clock, the light falling fast; soon it would be too late. I thought I might get an offer below the pool where the water was a little faster so, keeping low and quiet, I made my way downstream.

If I had an offer I mustn't miss it. It would soon be dark and I was cold. Slipping another shot on the line I cast across stream, placed one finger over the line with eyes on the rod top.

The lead rolled a few inches then, almost mesmerised, I watched the rod pull slowly over. I struck and a heavy fish bored in the current. The swim was snaggy and to keep contact I thrust the rod top under water. Slowly I gained line, then, with three pounds of chub wallowing on the surface, I slipped the net under him. Never have I been so thankful to see a fish in my net!

Two months later the film was shown. The following day I was approached by a non-angler. 'Saw you on telly last night,' he said, 'you made easy work of that. Next time they should give you something more difficult.' Ah, well.

12. Tench

My first 'real' experience with tench took place in Ireland. Until then I had caught tench from a wide variety of waters but due to the waters I fished, most were of average size – three to four pounds. Not that it bothered me, for I seldom fished for big tench; I was just happy catching them.

In 1958 I spent a holiday at John Roberts' hotel at Reynella, Co. Westmeath. John had his own lake which held some big tench. It wasn't an easy water to fish, however, for it was extremely weedy and shallow. At one end it deepened a little with bulrushes growing several feet out from the bank. It looked 'tenchy', and, if I remember rightly, caught the rays of the evening sun. Anyway, on the second evening we fished there and I quickly discovered what a good swim it was – providing that you knew when to strike.

I started off with bread paste, with the float shotted so that just the tip showed above the surface, with the shots stopped about 8 in. from the bait. The first evening was spent staring at bites – if you could call them that – which were nothing more than sharp 'knocks' on the float, indications one would expect from shy-biting roach. For some time I did nothing (don't ask me why) but eventually, in desperation, I struck at a 'knock' and to my surprise hooked a good tench. For the remainder of our stay this was the general pattern – I don't think I caught one tench which took the float under. Plenty of the tench topped four pounds, the best almost five.

That fortnight we had glorious weather (most un-Irish!) and one afternoon John Roberts demonstrated the art of catching tench under a blazing sun. As I said, the lake was very weedy, and on this particular day tench were lying almost stationary on top of the weed. I thought they were uncatchable

– but John quickly dispelled that idea. He pinched a piece of soft paste on to a No. 8 hook – nothing else was on the line – and cast well beyond a tench; he then gently wound it in towards, and in front of, the fish. As the bait drew level with the fish John stopped winding and allowed the paste to sink. The tench immediately showed interest, upended, and took the bait. I have since adopted the method with success on my waters.

I returned the following year (the little 'knocks' still persisted), but here my story switches to another lake close to Mullingar. Frank Guttfield, two others and I had fished this lake the previous year and had taken two 100-lb. bags. I decided to give it another try – this time at night.

Due to wide marginal rushes, most of the lake was unfishable; there were, I should think, less than half a dozen swims. I was therefore disappointed to find an angler fishing from the 'hot-spot' of the previous year. Sport, he told me, was poor, and I was not surprised, for he was fishing close in; tactics, which on our previous visit had proved fruitless. The lake was shallow, with an average depth of three feet, and the fish we had caught had been taken 30 yards out from the bank.

We had come for the night; how much longer, I wondered, would our friend stay? I liked to be settled in before dark and the sun had already set. We sat behind him waiting patiently. Suddenly he packed, we bade him good night, and once he had disappeared over the hill we moved into his swim.

I tackled up with a 6-lb. b.s. line, one swan shot on a sliding link and a No. 10 hook. Although I had brought both worms and bread I settled for soft paste, and after introducing a few small handfuls of soaked breadcrumbs, settled down.

The swim did not lend itself to float fishing. The bank – like those of many Irish lakes – was soft, and the slightest movement sent miniature waves across the water. The fish were, without doubt, well out. I don't often leger for tench, but here it was necessary. Casting with one shot wasn't easy, but although two would have changed this, I wanted the bait to sink as slowly as possible.

Our baits were cast, the rods placed in rests, and, pinching paste 'dollys' on the lines, we settled down. 'Settled' was hardly right – at least as far as I was concerned – for less than a minute had passed when my 'dolly' hit the rod butt with a resounding 'thud'.

Due to the shallow water the tench did not bore as tench normally do, but indulged in long, fast runs, and after making two or three runs straight for the middle, turned sideways towards the rushes. Maximum sidestrain was necessary in order to prevent disaster, and many anxious moments passed before the fish was netted. I popped him into the net and cast again.

A bite occurred immediately. I had not moved my hands from the dolly when it shot upwards. Fish number two. This occurred on the next cast, the next, and the next. Sport was now hectic, with tench after tench coming to the net – long, thin fish, yet in good condition. Sometimes the 'dolly' would twitch two or three times before bumping the rod, but all the bites were decisive and easy to hook.

Fish were now coming so fast that I was spending all my time either landing or unhooking them. I was covered with slime and many times I didn't have time to put the 'dolly' on the line. Why I persisted in doing so I don't know, for I could have easily held the rod and hooked those tench.

Yet, as so often happens when tench fishing, one man was catching the fish, Alan fishing alongside was fishless. But the fault did not lie with him or his tackle; it was just one of those unexplainable things that all tench fishermen have experienced.

Still the fish came. Many were lost, for they all made very fast runs towards the rushes and turning them was not easy. Finer tackle would have never held them; they were akin to miniature carp.

Darkness came and I suddenly realised that my dolly was not moving. Five minutes had passed without a bite – and a five-minute wait was unheard of in this particular water! But I was not worried, for even if the night proved fruitless there was still the dawn and the hours immediately following.

The night passed quietly without incident. Dawn broke and in the half light the bite indicator moved towards the butt ring.

As I struck another hard-fighting tench broke surface 20 yards out. But that was all; the sun rose, and by 8 a.m. it was warm. With half-closed eyes and heavy legs we packed, a trifle disappointed. As we trudged up the long hill to the car I couldn't help wondering how many we 'lost' by having to wait for our friend to pack the previous evening.

My catch was twenty-three fish, almost identical in size, the whole lot tipping the scales at 75 lb. Not big fish really – indeed they may well have been stunted – but their numbers and fighting qualities compensated for that.

In 1968 I joined a club which rented three large gravel pits. Now, in my district, good tench fishing – by 'good' I mean where four-pounders are common – are difficult to find, and I had never bothered to travel to find any. According to reports, the tench in these pits were of good size, and Fred Towns and I decided to have a go.

We arrived one morning at dawn, but at 10 a.m. we hadn't had a bite. There was little sign of tench bubbling (due to the hard bottom), but plenty were rolling. My float was lying under a shallow some four feet out from the bank in three feet of water, with a large piece of crust on the bottom. The surface was a flat calm – and I was fed up. More unlike tench conditions it would be hard to find – at least that is what I thought – but at that time my experience of tench in gravel pits was nil. I now know that in such waters hot, calm days can be very productive.

Anyway, there I was, thinking of packing, when the float shot under – no preliminaries – it just went. Four and a quarter pounds. I cast again, placed the rod in the rests, the float disappeared, the rod bent round almost shooting into the water and I struck (don't know why) – all in three seconds flat! Four and a half pounds. Two more quickly followed, four and three quarters and four pounds fourteen ounces. Four four-pounders – I was dead chuffed!

That season my tally of four-pound tench grew with every visit, and Fred took his share too. One morning he caught one five-and-a-quarter, with a two-pound roach to keep it company

– lucky devil! Also important was the fact that a pattern quickly emerged; the behaviour of those tench, and the 'magic' feeding hour.

Certainly the tench were cruisers. Unlike tench in muddy-bottomed lakes they did not remain in one spot for long. I formed this opinion because bites on both lobs and paste (these proved the most successful baits, although maggots fished on fine tackle – 3-lb. b.s. line and No. 16 hooks – proved best once August arrived) were decisive, the float either shooting under out of sight without warning or, when legering, line leaping off the spool. And bites came in spasms; you might catch five fish in as many minutes, then nothing for an hour. It appeared they swam around in shoals picking up food as they roamed. Very seldom did long feeding periods occur. Once a tench found the bait it was taken with confidence: those tench were hungry fish.

Point number two was the time when bites were most frequent. Dawn would find the tench already rolling well out, with a few close in. On one occasion it rained and a gale blew – in my book good tench conditions – and I took four good fish four hours after arrival. Norman Woodward, who knows a thing or two about tench, wrote once on this subject and said that 7 a.m. was early enough to be abroad. My knowledge of big tench isn't as great as Norman's, and I would disagree with this time for some lakes. But not in my pit, and anglers fishing nearby pits have confirmed this. We rarely caught much before 7 a.m.

On the morning of June 16th, 1970 Fred, John Everard and I fished the pits again and made what one angling paper called 'a piece of angling history'. We hadn't fished this pit before, but a close-season 'recce' revealed it to be full of fish. We decided to make it our opening day venue.

I must admit that Fred and John did all the work. For a month they pre-baited three swims, with a lot of travelling involved. In early June the swim, most evenings, was boiling with fish, and on the evening of the World Cup Final I went too – just at the start of extra time! I was amazed at what I saw;

the swim wasn't just boiling – it was a flipping cauldron! I could hardly wait.

We arrived on the evening of the 15th, tackled up and made ourselves comfy. The 'cauldron' was still boiling; seldom, if ever, have I seen so many fish in one swim. By 9.30 p.m. we were impatient – as were other club members situated at other parts of the pit.

'How much longer?' asked John. 'Two and a half hours,' Fred replied, 'This waiting is killing me.' 'Think I'll find the right depth, then I'm ready,' John muttered, and I watched him cast his unbaited hook into the water and make adjustments to the float. 'Did you see that?' John said excitedly. 'I had a bite – and I've got no bait on.' I smiled, but John was adamant; he *had* seen his float move. 'I'll try again,' he said. I watched his float cock then slide slowly under. A minute later John netted a three-pound tench hooked fairly in the mouth.

We were expecting a heavy bag of tench; now we knew we were in for an exceptional catch, and the swirling and rolling fish showed just how effective the pre-baiting had been.

But despite the activity, three factors worried me. Firstly, had the tench become evening feeders, had we, by pre-baiting in the evenings, conditioned them into feeding at that time? If so, our midnight start might be too late. Secondly, we would be fishing with a light shining on the float, and two anglers had taken up position on an island to our left: a badly directed torch with the beam piercing the water instead of skimming it, would certainly ruin our chances. Or would it? – read Chapter 16. Thirdly, the moon was full, and I've rarely caught fish on moonlight nights. Whilst I pondered on this, tench continued to swirl and roll in our swims with rods lying in the rests doing nothing. We were three very frustrated fishermen, and John catching that tench on a bare hook didn't help matters.

Finally I could stand it no longer: there were, I admit, a few minutes still to go before midnight, but I consoled myself by saying that perhaps my watch was slow. Three carefully positioned torches were turned on simultaneously, their beams only inches above the surface, followed by three 'plops' as our baits (breadcrust) touched the water. Within three seconds – no more – Fred and John were into fish, whilst I missed one. Two torches to our left were quickly turned on, their beams, thankfully, above the water. Against the night sky I could see Fred's rod bending, whilst a screaming clutch to my left told me that John was into another. Little did we realise it then, but this was the prelude to a fantastic night's fishing.

During the next four hours there was always one rod bending, most of the time two, and on four occasions, all three. And we had our quota of laughs too. Around 1 a.m. Fred, in his haste to re-cast, got a lovely 'birdsnest'. With fish rolling all around him, a torch which would persist in falling over, two mates who were clobbering tench every cast saying things like 'Hurry up, Fred, they are going mad,' his troubles got progressively worse. I fished on, hoping that no courting couples were within earshot, for Fred's language was, at times, very choice indeed.

The fish were of good average size, ranging between two and four pounds, with several 'knocking on' for five. And what scrappers too! I hooked one fish which took line at an alarming rate and full pressure failed to stop it. 'Carp,' I said (and hoped for), but when the fish finally stopped running I guessed it was another tench, but foulhooked. And so it proved, a two-pounder hooked in the tail. A disappointing fish.

The next fish I knew was a good 'un, for it bored deep and heavy. I applied pressure and, to my surprise, the fish kept going. My finger pressed on the spool even tighter; still I couldn't stop him. I tightened the tension nut – or thought I did – but more line was taken. In the light of the moon I peered at the reel – the tension nut was missing. This was serious. Here I was with a very good fish and little means of controlling it. Pressing the line against the rod I stopped him and slowly recovered line with my other hand. I wasn't sorry when I finally steered the fish over the net; a good fish which turned the scales at $5\frac{1}{4}$ lb.

Half an hour later I did a 'Fred'. Bullying a medium-sized fish, the hook pulled out and everything landed behind me in a truly horrible mess. I immediately cut the line, but tackling up in darkness with a torch between your knees, trying to find the 'split' in a split shot with clutches screaming either side of you is not good on the nerves. When I finally sat down, re-organised at last, I thought again of courting couples. I hoped none were around, although after Fred's blast-off it was extremely doubtful.

At 3.30 a.m. dawn broke. In the distance a cockerel crowed, a heron glided ghost-like overhead and a cuckoo let us know it wasn't far away. Half an hour later we turned off the torches, and as we did so the bites ceased – just like that. In the next three hours just one tench fell to our rods.

We lifted the five large keepnets from the water. The task of counting, weighing and photographing the catch was, however, too much, for we were fishing from a spit of land immediately under a high bank. John counted his – forty-seven – whilst Fred and I each had over thirty, so our combined weight certainly topped 250 lb. – possibly more. Several fish were over four pounds, topped by two very good fish of 5 lb. 5 oz. and 5 lb. 4 oz., of which John took one and I the other.

Three very tired but happy anglers, trudged back to the cars, nets reeking of slime, and trousers in need of washing. Two hundred and fifty pounds – what a start to a season!

Whilst 'tinca' has long been associated with lakes and ponds, I much, much prefer to seek them in gravel-pits, especially those containing little or no weed. Without weed to hamper the angler (who in consequence can use finer tackle than he normally would) they not only fight longer and better, but also feed for longer periods – often throughout the day in brilliant sunshine. As a rule, no matter what the weather – and that includes high winds – they will feed, and feed well. Those who say – plenty still do – that tench feed best when 'the mist rises from the water foretelling the hot presently' haven't done much tench fishing.

13. Annan chub

Ever since the reputed 10½ lb. record chub was taken from the Annan I had cherished an ambition to fish the river. Not that I expected to catch a double-figure chub – if indeed such fish were present; just that, having heard so much about the river and its potential, I had to go and see for myself.

In the summer of 1967 my wife and I spent two weeks' holiday in Dumfries, with the intention (amongst other things) of finding out a little about this famous river. Long before our trip I made enquiries about the fishing which, of course, is strictly salmon and trout. Further enquiries finally resulted in my obtaining permission to try for the coarse fish, so imagine my joy when a permit for a week's fishing eventually arrived. I arrived in Dumfries eagerly awaiting my first glimpse of the river.

Sunday fishing is prohibited in most waters in Scotland, the Annan being no exception, and it was Monday before I could get cracking. First impressions were good; shallows, alternating with deeps and full of character, winding and fast. I didn't like the colour very much though – a dark, peaty colour which would, I thought, seriously reduce my chances of observing chub on the surface; a suspicion later to be proved correct. Nevertheless, I had a feeling that it was only a matter of locating the chub, the rest would be easy.

By pure chance the first angler I spoke to was the bailiff. I informed him of my interest in the chub, an interest which he couldn't understand. But what a helpful chap he turned out to be. Further down river, he informed me, was a large pool, a pool unfished by salmon anglers because of the large numbers of chub present. Most reaches of the river were, he said, poisoned from time to time to remove the coarse fish; this particular pool, however, was never touched.

I enquired about the reputed ten-pounder. He had apparently seen the fish which, he assured me, *was* a chub. But that was not all: they had, from time to time, taken double-figure chub when poisoning the river; not many it was true, but a few.

Now I'm always a little sceptical about people who speak freely about outsize fish, so I asked him what size of chub I could expect downstream in the pool. 'Two pounds,' he replied, 'but there are plenty of five-and six-pounders if you can catch them.' This statement sounded honest enough, and with hopes high Sue and I got into the car and headed for the pool.

Eventually we found the river again, left the car and made the rest of the journey on foot. It was a very hot afternoon, with the sun blazing down, and I sweated under my load of tackle. I had come well prepared with a large supply of lobworms and loaves of bread, for, although I didn't think the actual bait would be important, I considered that plenty might be necessary.

Suddenly we found the pool, a big one quite seventy yards across. But that was not all. Along the margins were countless numbers of bow-waves caused by cruising fish. Seldom have I witnessed such a sight; the water was literally boiling with them. We approached the water carefully, for the bank was low and soggy, shaking as we walked over it. Next day I was to find out why.

With trembling hands I tackled up – a 6-lb. b.s. line, No. 6 hook and a small float two inches in length carrying one swan shot. This I pushed against the float which I stopped two feet from the hook. On this I placed a large lob.

The bait hit the water and the fish scattered. They were some time in returning but they did, and five minutes later the float cocked and slid away. I struck, hooked the fish, a big 'boil' and he was gone. Obviously they needed more time, and I cast again. This time I let the float travel a little longer, a gentle strike and he was on. After a very good scrap I netted him – my first Annan chub. And what a beautiful fish; not weight-wise perhaps – after all I can catch $3\frac{1}{2}$ lb. chub at home

– but the colouring – bright red fins and bronze body with not a blemish on it. 'I've never seen such a lovely fish,' Sue remarked as I placed it in the keepnet.

Still the bow-waves continued, the place was alive with chub. Despite all that, however, I couldn't get another bite, and I had a feeling that the float was responsible. Although the fish were not used to hooks, they still retained their cunning and shyness – even more so in fact. Obviously a change of tactics was necessary.

I removed both float and shot, leaving just the hook on the line with a large lob attached. This I cast as far as I could, then retrieved it in short jerks. That did the trick. The first cast produced a four-pounder, quickly followed by several others, all around the three-pound mark. Then, suddenly, the bites stopped, also the activity, and all went quiet. With tea at six and a journey ahead of us, we packed.

Before I departed, however, I crawled to the area where most of the activity had taken place. Two chub glided out from the shallows. I will not guess their weight, but I know that just one of them would have been enough to make my journey worthwhile.

That evening we returned. It was still hot but a change had come over the swim. Apart from one huge fish that bolted from the shallows (it couldn't have been a chub that size – or could it?), I saw, and caught, nothing. As we packed, rain began to fall.

We awoke next morning to find it still raining. Undaunted, we made our way over to the pool. What a change had taken place. On the quickly rising river the pool was twice its size, and where we had sat the previous day fish were now rising. Swirls and leaping chub covered almost the entire area, sometimes as many as six fish showing at the same time.

From my bank a strong wind blew towards me, and a shot pinched on the line was necessary to get the bait out. Once this had touched bottom I let out a little slack, and watched the line as it hung from the rod top. There was no mistaking a bite; the line would tighten rapidly, the chub almost hooking themselves. In the shallow water (even in this 'flood' I couldn't find 4 ft. of water), the fish fought like demons, and only by holding the rod very low to prevent undue splashing could I avoid disturbing them too much.

Mid-way through the afternoon I began to have doubts about catching a big one. I had, by this time, got ten in the net – all between 2½ lb. and 3½ lb. With the fish still rising I moved from my swim to another fifty yards away. Here, however, it was the same story. I took five more of the same size before tea-time, when we made our way home.

The next day was much the same, although the pool had dropped to its original level. Rain threatened all day – one of those dark, cheerless days – with a cold wind blowing. Using the same tactics I took fourteen, all round the 3-lb. mark. I returned home thinking what I should do the following day – the last on which I could fish.

Again it rained all night, and it was still drizzling when we arrived. 'What a way to spend a holiday, under an umbrella,' Sue remarked – God bless her, she never grumbles. The pool was again twice its size, and still the strong wind persisted.

This time I would try something different. On previous visits I had decided against groundbaiting – with so many fish present I did not see its purpose – today, however, I would try. Choosing an area previously unfished, I introduced two handfuls into a swim forty yards from the bank. I would also give them a different bait – breadcrust and flake.

I took four fish – three-pounders – when a big chub boiled on the surface. Were they surface feeders I wondered? I quickly changed to float tackle, trotting the bait down the pool just below the surface. Still I caught fish, but alas, no different in size. This was no good; I had to get a big one. Picking up my gear I took the long walk to the other side of the pool which I had not fished. To my amazement the plummet revealed 20 ft. of water right under the bank with barely 6 ft. not twenty yards out.

I fished the deeps, the middle and the surrounding area. Still the fish came, not quickly mind, but regularly. But these, too, were like peas in a pod, with nothing above 3½ lb. With the fish still biting freely – how many I could have caught had I really put my mind to it I don't know – I packed, slightly disappointed despite another good bag.

So ended my long-awaited trip to the Annan. In one way a disappointing one, for I had hoped for at least one big fish. On the other hand it was first-class sport and, had I really tried, I believe 100 lb. at a sitting was possible. But that's not quite like one big one.

What are the chances of a monster Annan chub? Fair I would say, certainly possible. My only regret was I could not stay longer, for I longed to try another reach where the chub were not so numerous. I think the swim I fished held too many chub to make the capture of a big one possible without a huge slice of luck.

The ideal situation, of course, would be to find the river low and clear (if indeed it does get clear), with the sun beating down; then, I think it might be possible to see an outsize chub and show it a bait; that, I think, would give one a good chance, but it only needs a drop of rain to send the river soaring. Unfortunately, I only found it in that mood once – the first afternoon – otherwise I might be telling a different story.

14. Royalty barbel

Everyone has either seen or heard of the Royalty fishery on the Hampshire Avon. The first time I fished the water was during the summer of 1962, when Pete Drennan and I spent a weekend with Bill and Sonny Warren, whose Royalty catches are legendary.

On the Saturday we took our first look at the water. Bill told us to leger with large lumps of cheese behind a salmon stone immediately below the Pipe Bridge. 'Don't strike at nibbles or half-hearted pulls,' Bill said, 'wait until the rod pulls right round.' This surprised me rather, but there, who was I to argue with Bill on Royalty matters?

For two hours I was bothered with 'knocks' and 'jabs' on the rod top, but I did nothing. Then Bill arrived. 'Can't get a pull Bill,' I said, 'are you *sure* I shouldn't strike these little knocks and jabs?' But Bill was adamant, so, being the good boy, I did nothing.

After a while Bill announced he was going home to tea. 'I'll be back in an hour,' he said, 'to show you how to catch one.' Bill's back was hardly turned when yet another little 'knock' came to the rod top. I struck and the rod pulled over. I was into my first Avon barbel.

I then learnt something else; not to use weights like Arlesey Bombs when legering behind boulders. As I struck, the weight became jammed under the boulder and all went solid. Climbing on to the high bank I could see the barbel – a good one – rolling over in the current with me helpless. Thankfully the barbel eventually came off, and I pulled for a break. Following that little incident I decided to strike at anything which looked like a bite, which later resulted in Pete and I catching some nice barbel and chub.

Soon after, Bill returned. 'Come and try the Rushes swim,' he said, 'bound sure to get one there.' The swim was upstream of the bridge, the river a mass of ranunculus with a very small channel running down the centre. The bank was thickly lined with rushes (hence its name), and the only possible way to fish it was to leger upstream in the narrow channel. This entailed a fairly long, accurate cast using a trail of three feet. The bait was cheese.

'Now then,' Bill said, 'give me the rod and I'll show you what to do.' Placing an enormous piece of cheese on the No. 6 hook, Bill cast into the channel. The line sunk, he took up the slack, struck, and pressing the rod into my hand, said 'land it' – just like that! Two minutes later I had him out – $10\frac{1}{4}$ lb.

I quickly re-baited and cast to the top of the channel. Taking up the slack I watched the line fall slack, struck – and felt nothing.

Now this often happens when upstream legering; the fish picks up the bait and swims downstream very fast; the line drops but the angler only strikes slack line. What you do is this. Immediately following the strike you point the rod quickly at the water, at the same time winding in, then strike again.

I hooked the fish on the second strike. Then disaster. When only feet from the bank the barbel came off, a fish most certainly in double figures.

I fished the 'Rushes' for several years following, and although I never had a 'double' I had plenty just under. Not only was it a fascinating swim to fish but, because it looked formidable, most anglers passed it by.

In 1965 I fished the Royalty again when everyone was fishing maggots on fine tackle. One evening I watched two anglers lumping out barbel to $11\frac{1}{4}$ lb. immediately above the Railway Bridge. A dense patch of ranunculus reached from bank to bank, but where it ended – at the point where the shallows met deeps – the barbel were feeding. They were congregated under the weed and occasionally drifted back downstream to feed. The anglers were 'laying on' with maggots.

Naturally (this was the Royalty, remember) you had to be there very early to get the swim (on one occasion a chap stayed all night!), but one day Peter Wheat got it. That day Pete took a large bag, including two over ten pounds, and I noticed that he took most of them during the evening.

Two boys from Sheffield fished it the following day and, as I had booked up a sea trip, I didn't go until late evening. The boys were very despondent, for they were fishless. I felt really sorry for them, and asked whether they intended fishing it the next day. 'No fear,' they said, 'we've had enough.'

They eventually packed, and I moved into the swim and did something I have never done before or since: I 'booked' a swim. Fixing up a brolly I placed two buckets under it and left a rod in a rest. In the darkness it looked just as if someone was fishing, but I wasn't – and didn't intend to either. I went back to my 'digs' and went to bed!

I arrived next morning whilst it was still dark, waited until it got light, then started fishing. To fish meant standing in two feet of water, so I waded out with a bucketful of maggots around my waist and a bait dropper on a spare rod. My float carried two swan shot and the hook was a No. 12, the line 5-lb. b.s. The float was set so it laid at half-cock.

First cast I was into one; a sharp 'dig' on the float and he was away! 8 lb. dead. Before I could get it in the net, however, a chap waded out and planted himself no more than four feet from me. I told him what I thought, but it was some time before he moved, still maintaining he had a right to be there! I don't like rows and it put me off for a bit, but I eventually copped another, also around the 8-lb. mark. 'Must get a double,' I said to myself, 'just a matter of time.'

Funnily enough, I didn't get any more bites, and by teatime my bag was just eight fish, all between six and eight and a half pounds. It was enjoyable fishing though; a bait dropper filled with maggots would bring them around and the float lying at half-cock behind the weed would either suddenly shoot under, or give a sharp 'dig'. Then came the fight – and for once those Royalty barbel *did* fight.

At 6 p.m. I did a very silly thing indeed; I can't think why, but I did. Peter Wheat had warned me that, although they fed steadily all day, there was one period lasting about an hour when they went mad. The two Sheffield boys had been watching me all day so I invited them to fish the swim whilst I went and had some tea. I gave them my tackle and left them to it.

An hour later Sue and I returned. The lads were very excited. Whilst I had been away they had hooked and lost twelve fish – Peter's 'magic hour'. I cursed and swore and swore again!

Now, whether they had upset the swim or not I don't know, but I couldn't get another bite. But Sue, legering six feet away, could – and how. I stood and watched as her rod top pulled over and finally she hooked one. Then the fun *really* started.

This barbel was most certainly a 'double'. Sue played it quite well, but the tension on her reel was too slack, so I reached over to tighten it. As I did so my finger touched the line – and bang it went. Sadly I watched it slide through the rod rings then, as it reached the top ring it tangled and Sue found herself connected to it once more.

Telling her to hold the rod tightly I threaded the line through the rings again then, as I reached the tip ring told her to slacken off. The barbel was most obliging – it slackened off too! I undid the tangle and tied the two ends with a blood knot. I clipped the ends and told her to tighten again. The fish was still on.

But our joy was shortlived; it gave one run and the line fell slack – the hook had come adrift.

Still, Sue continued to hook barbel whilst I continued watching a motionless float. I finally packed with just the eight fish but not one 'double'. A good day, yes, but it should have been much, much better, for I disregarded Peter's warning. Nevertheless, I think I was unlucky not to get a big one; apart from the two lads, I must have been the only angler that week who didn't.

Several years have now passed since I last fished the Royalty, and it will be a long time, I fear, before I do so again. Petty restrictions, bans – and other things – have resulted in a 'fairground' fishery in which I am not interested.

A far cry indeed from the 'Bill Warren era'. I'm pleased I knew those days – if only for a short while. What fishing: and the 'Rushes' swim too, the likes of which I shall never know again.

15. 1963 Freeze-up

It was January 1963 and we were experiencing one of the most cruel winters on record. From my window I could see the ice-covered lake, on a normal Saturday busy with anglers, now completely deserted. Across the ice walked hungry moorhens, the pattern of their footsteps plainly visible in the snow. An east wind blew across the garden, and the thermometer indicated that the temperature was well below freezing. Yet, despite all that, I was going fishing.

The bitter weather had been with us three weeks, three weeks of intense cold. The snow had fallen one Saturday night and I awoke next morning to find the village deep in it, so deep in fact that I was unable to find my way to the river. That day I didn't fish, being content to walk – or rather stumble – through the snow admiring the wonderful scenery.

The following weekend I went fishing; not for long mind you – even I found it too cold! Immediately below a small weir-pool I found a bit of clear water where a few chub, roach and bream – yes, bream – obliged. By the third weekend everywhere was frozen solid and I actually walked along the Thames into Oxford. But walking wasn't enough; I wanted to fish, and fish I would.

A quick check with Ted confirmed that he too was game; a short walk through the village, and we were at the river. On the way down a jovial character shouted across the road, 'You will have to break the ice today.' Little did he realise it, but that was precisely what we intended doing! Rows of willows lined the bank; here the ice would not be too thick. Finding a large branch, we managed to break a hole about a yard square and, with fingers already numbed, we tackled up.

My tackle consisted of a 3-lb. b.s. line, a float carrying one small shot and a No. 16 hook. On this I put one maggot. By this time a thin layer of ice had formed over the hole; this I broke and scooped out with the landing net. I then introduced some maggots and lowered my bait into the hole.

The float was shotted so that only half an inch showed above the surface. Almost immediately I noticed a movement, so slight it was barely discernible – a tiny 'ring', nothing more. I struck, expecting a small fish, but the tackle stayed put! Slowly a heavy fish bored down deeply under the ice and I was forced to give line. Quickly I thrust the rod top under water to prevent the ice cutting the line, and gently played the fish in that position. Eventually I surfaced him – a chub of three pounds. I pulled his head on to the ice, the rest quickly followed, and I slid him over to the bank. Another small hole was broken against the bank to house the keepnet, more maggots were thrown into the hole, I then re-baited and cast again.

This time I had to wait a little longer, by which time ice was forming round the float. This I broke, tapping it gently with the rod top. The ripples had barely died away when another tiny 'ring' appeared round the float. A second later I was playing another heavy chub, again with the rod top under water. Three and a half pounds.

An hour later I decided to move. There were now five chub in the net, but I hadn't had a bite for some time. I found Ted some way upstream; he, too, had made himself a hole but, apart from one fish which had broken him (he had forgotten to put his rod top under the water) he hadn't had a bite. Ted was using cheese on leger tackle, which, in the circumstances, I considered wrong.

I forced another hole upstream of Ted and adopted the same procedure as before. Once again I caught a chub immediately I started fishing, which was quickly followed up by three more. The chub were biting and taking the single maggot almost as soon as the float had settled but, due to the intense cold, I was missing bites. I didn't like the thought of packing up with the fish going so well, yet I knew I couldn't take much more. Just time, I thought, to have another cast in my original swim. Again the branch came into play, and the whole procedure of removing the ice was gone through again. Two more chub were the result of my labours then, with the icy air really clamping down, we called it a day. Eleven chub plus one from Ted was the total; a truly interesting day.

For several weeks we broke the ice, fished until we were frozen; caught fish, good fish too – and thoroughly enjoyed ourselves! Each visit taught us things about fish and their habits in arctic conditions; knowledge which has since stood us in good stead.

The first signs of a thaw came towards the end of one week. Ted and I journeyed to the river on the Saturday and for the first time in weeks found a strip of clear water on the edge of a weirpool large enough to accommodate three anglers. I looked at the swim, liked the look of it, and decided to try.

Another brave soul was already fishing. Our enquiry revealed that he hadn't had a bite, but this didn't worry me unduly. I had a feeling that the chub would be lying just under the ice, and that a bait rolled down the clear water to them might be taken. The other angler was fishing twenty yards upstream of the icepack.

I positioned myself a few yards upstream of where the clear water met the solid ice, introduced a couple of handfuls of soaked breadcrumbs and settled down. My tackle was 6-lb. b.s. line, a No. 8 hook on, bait cheese-paste. Three 'swans' on a sliding link rolled bottom nicely, and I cast so that my bait rolled gently round, eventually coming to rest just to my side of the solid ice.

I was jarred to my senses by the rod almost being pulled from my hands; I struck and missed. The next cast produced a similar bite, and that one I landed. Meanwhile, Ted fishing alongside was also getting big pulls – and missing them. Within an hour I copped several nice chub, two of which topped four pounds; a poor reward really, considering the opportunities presented. Eventually, due to the cold, we packed.

That day I made a big mistake by using cheese-paste. As I said, every bite was a big pull, bites which are difficult to hit. The trouble lay in the cheese hardening in the water; the fish were picking up the bait and bolting with it – hence the big pulls. But a small piece of crust or flake would, I know, have resulted in smaller, but better bites, bites which we would have hooked. But I had no bread, only cheese-paste. I should have known better.

Throughout the following week the thaw continued, although snow was still thick on the ground. By the Saturday the scene had changed considerably; the ice had now broken up, and the weirpool was a mass of miniature ice-bergs. Fishing was almost impossible. The 'ice-bergs' were bad enough; worse still, ice was melting in the water. Only rarely, in my experience, do fish feed in such conditions.

But I fished – or at least I held a line in the water, for it was difficult to prevent the 'bergs from fouling the line. But I knew where the fish were; against a small ledge just out from the bank. On a No. 10 hook I placed a small piece of crust (I hadn't forgotten it this time) and cast into the area. Holding the rod high I watched the line at the point it entered the water, not so much for bite detection but so that I could guide the line clear of the pack ice that continually floated past.

After a while I felt a sharp 'knock' on the line, struck, and found myself into a nice fish. I had quite a game with him, keeping a tight line at the same time as dodging the ice packs, but I managed it, and eventually landed a nice four-pounder.

An hour later I had another 'knock'. I knew it was no chub but I certainly didn't expect a three-pound bream! Two bites – two fish; a few pictures, and I was soon indoors enjoying the comforts of the fireside. On reflection, I think those were the worse conditions I have ever fished in.

The next day I fished again, this time for pike. Close to where I had fished the previous day was a narrow channel of clear water along a backwater. This reach held a large head of pike, and Fred Smith and I decided to have a try. We caught some live-baits (no fun that, I can tell you) and were soon fishing.

For over three hours we never had a bite. Then, quite suddenly, a blizzard – and that's an understatement – blew up. In less than a minute visibility was almost nil and it was very, very cold indeed. I decided to pack, and as I retrieved my tackle from the water a pike grabbed the bait. I caught him – an eight-pounder I think it was – so, despite the howling wind and driving snow I dipped my hands into the bait bucket (a cold job that!) grabbed another bait and cast again. As the float settled it shot under and a minute later another pike was flapping in the snow.

Fred, fishing alongside, was also having fun. Whilst the blizzard raged the pike fed ravenously; often we were playing fish together. The cold was forgotten – well, almost – as with numbed fingers we fought the pike. Then, quite suddenly, the blizzard stopped and, strangely enough, so did the bites. We didn't have another run. A strange, but frantic half-hour.

By the following weekend the thaw was complete; the freeze-up was over. Now, as I write, the wind howls outside and 1963 seems a long time ago. A cruel winter; the like of which one hopes we shall never see again. A winter, though, in which I learned so much.

16. *A gravel pit*

I first met John Everard in 1969. John, a shy, unassuming chap, had several big fish to his credit, and he had fished waters many of which I had never seen – or even heard of. 'Ever fished that pit at H . . . ?' he asked me one day, 'It holds some good fish – including chub.' I didn't know the water, so John took me along to have a look. Little did I know it then, but I was looking at a water which was to provide me with not only many big fish, but also some of the happiest experiences I have spent fishing.

The first time I fished I caught a few chub; nothing very large but, as my experience of still-water chub was almost nil, I decided to devote most of that season to them. The next few outings resulted in more chub, most of which were caught on legered crust. It was good fishing and I became more and more interested in the pit.

One evening John fished it alone and caught a roach weighing $1\frac{3}{4}$ lb. The next evening he caught one that was two ounces heavier. But that was not all; more roach were sighted – all big ones – some over two pounds.

Now there is nothing I like more than catching big roach on fine tackle, and the pit lent itself to fine lines and small hooks. John had seen these roach close in so I laid plans accordingly: to fish with small pieces of bread on a No. 14 hook tied to a 3-lb. b.s. line. I selected some very small floats carrying two B.B. shot and awaited my next opportunity.

One July evening, Fred Towns phoned to say he was going over. Would I join him? I didn't need asking twice, and we arranged to meet there in an hour. The air was close and humid – good roach conditions. I had some tea, packed my gear and was just off when it started to rain. And how! Not wishing

A GRAVEL PIT

to fish in a downpour I phoned Fred's wife to cancel the trip. 'He's just gone,' Jean said, 'you've only just missed him.' Not wishing to let Fred down, I set off. Secretly I cursed Fred; why, I thought, must he go fishing in such weather? I eventually arrived at the pit and found Fred huddled under his brolly. No bites had been forthcoming, which didn't surprise me.

I decided to fish about 100 yards from Fred, where John had seen a shoal of roach. For some unknown reason I decided to fish well out in 5 ft. of water. I tackled up with an antenna float carrying three A.A. shot and squeezed a piece of flake on to a No. 14 hook.

By now the rain had eased to a steady drizzle and the air was very, very warm. Had I been bream fishing I would have said conditions were perfect – but on reflection they probably were, as you will see later. I started getting bites straight away, bites which pulled the float down very, very slowly until it almost sank, but not quite. If I struck I missed; if I left well alone nothing happened. This continued for two hours, during which time I caught nothing.

It was almost dark and still drizzling when, once again, the float almost sank. I struck and all went solid. As I increased pressure it moved – and how – for within seconds ten yards of line was stripped off the reel. Then it stopped and a great slab of silver – yes silver – rolled over on the surface. 'Bream Stoney!' I said aloud, 'a bloody great bream!'

I couldn't call the fight spectacular – more nerve-racking really – for every time it dived my rod shuddered as if someone had dropped a sandbag on the rod top. Dick Walker experienced this with his 44-lb. carp and like Dick, every time my fish dived – 'sounded' would be a better word – my heartbeat quickened. I could see it was a big fish and prayed the hook would hold.

Three minutes later I steered him over my net – the biggest bream I had ever seen alive. I called Fred who, like me, had never seen such a fish, and together we guessed its weight. Fred said eight, I seven. The scales stopped at $8\frac{1}{4}$ lb.

Its size apart, it was the most beautiful bream I had ever seen, short (23 in.), thick – and completely silver. I decided to have it set up, and it now occupies a place of honour above my bookcase.

Several questions concerning that capture remain. Were all the bites, on that damp, dismal evening (how thankful I was Fred went!) from bream; was I in fact fishing over a shoal of monsters? If so, why were they so difficult to hit? Were they in fact just holding the bait between their lips (my hook fell out before I could touch it)? Finally, to the best of our knowledge, no one has caught a bream there since.

Shortly after I entered hospital, during which time both Fred and John caught roach between $1\frac{1}{2}$ lb. and 1 lb. 14 oz. I eventually got fishing again, but couldn't catch them. Winter came, and although we could see roach in our swims they proved very, very difficult to catch.

One afternoon Fred J. Taylor and I had a shoal right under our feet feeding in less than three feet of water. Every time we threw in a handful of maggots they would rise off the bottom and take them as they were sinking. 'Simple,' I remember saying to Fred, 'show 'em a maggot on a No. 18 – that'll have 'em.' So I did just that – and my slowly sinking maggot was ignored. I finally scaled down to a No. 22 on 1-lb. b.s. line; still my maggot was ignored – after, I might say, a *very* close inspection. We just could *not* catch those roach 'on the drop,' and today, two years later, the situation hasn't changed.

That winter I caught a few roach to $1\frac{1}{2}$ lb., all on single maggot and No. 22 hook; to use anything larger meant no bites. Great care was necessary when a big roach was hooked for they always rose to the surface and swirled. If you held them too hard the hook would give, and I only got over this difficulty by removing all tension from my reel. Chub, despite their boring tactics, seldom came adrift but the swirling roach certainly posed a problem.

At first we thought that dusk would give us the best chance of roach, for, in every water I have fished, that final hour ('the last knockings') has always proved best. But not at our

A GRAVEL PIT

pit. This we couldn't understand and don't really today, although I think we know part of the answer. But more of that later.

In the 1970–71 close-season I made plans to catch those big roach; a small float carrying one 'dust', 2-lb. b.s. line and No. 22 hook on a 1-lb. 'point' fished close in, in swims where we could see them, *must*, I thought, succeed. I decided to go immediately the season opened and Fred, John and I made plans accordingly.

On the second night of the season my phone rang just as I was off to bed. It was Fred: 'would I like a photo of a big roach? if so, John had got one 2½ lb.' Within half an hour I was at the pit.

John was fishing a 'new' swim (for us) and had caught his roach soon after arrival. He had two others – both around the 1½-lb. mark – and had lost another. I photographed the fish then looked at his tackle. He was using a long antenna float carrying a No. 12 hook baited with bread. So much for my 22s and 1-lb. b.s. line!

Three days later Fred and John fished the same swim at dawn. I was prevented from getting there until midday and arrived to find them emptying their keepnets. I can't remember how many they had, but every fish topped the pound, Fred taking one of 2 lb. 2 oz. I could hardly wait to tackle up.

But I was doomed to disappointment; all I could catch were tench, perch and chub – no roach. Meanwhile, Fred and John, fishing alongside, caught more fish to 1¾ lb. I went home disappointed – and frustrated!

But not for long. On my next visit I caught several topping the pound but again the interesting thing was that dusk did not prove productive, whereas bright sunshine did not deter them. Both John and Fred caught a two-pounder plus several to 1 lb. 14 oz. But try as I did, I could not manage one of two pounds. And I badly wanted one.

Over the years I had caught a great number of roach to 1 lb. 15 oz., mainly from the Thames, which is not a 'big' roach water, but never a 'two'. Not that I hadn't caught roach that *should* have topped that weight. I remember a bag from the Tweed taken in front of the television cameras in company with Fred J. Taylor and Dick Walker, big roach which, unfortunately, had just spawned. And there was the really big roach I took from a gravel pit one night which should have weighed 2½ lb. At 1 lb. 12 oz. that fish was, I think, one of the most disappointing fish I have ever caught. But I am digressing.

One night we fished after dark with a light on the float. Our floats were fairly heavy with long antennas with an orange 'bulb' on the top. In the light of a cycle lamp these floats shone like stars in the night and were very easy to see. The antenna was painted black and white stripes; the fish only had to pull or lift the float ½ in. for the bite to register.

My word, how those roach fed once darkness descended. Mind you, the fishing wasn't *that* easy – what night fishing is? – but we caught good roach every time we went. Steadily our numbers of big roach grew, with Fred the 'champion' by a long chalk. One night he caught eighteen, with plenty of 'dozens' on other occasions – all good roach well over the pound. One evening Fred and I decided to see just how long they would feed, for with most of our fishing taking place in mid-week we couldn't fish too late because of work next day. Packing up with big roach biting freely wasn't easy I can tell you, but work came first; after all, the family can't live on roach!

True to form, they started feeding just after dark (dusk, as usual, was unproductive) and we started catching fish to 1 lb. 14 oz. Then, at 2 a.m., I came very close to making contact with another large bream. It came about like this.

Suddenly the roach stopped feeding and for over ten minutes our floats never moved – which was unusual to say the least! Well, I say 'never moved'; I'm not quite sure about that because at one stage I thought mine moved but wasn't sure. However, about ten minutes later I decided to re-cast. As I lifted the rod I felt a heavy resistance, then, as I increased pressure, the fish moved off very, very slowly. Suddenly there was a terrific 'thud' on the rod top – just like a sand-bag! This was followed by one more 'thud' then it was gone. I wound up to find my tackle *behind* me.

I was very annoyed about that because I have one golden rule; *always* strike, whether a bite has occurred or not. On that occasion I didn't, and I paid for it.

Five minutes later the roach returned and we continued catching them to 3 a.m. I forget what our bag was, but it doesn't matter; we had a good night. But that 'dead' fifteen minutes intrigued me most, for when bream enter a swim everything else appears to go. Yes, I am convinced a shoal paid us a visit that night and that I came very close indeed to catching one.

One hot, sunny morning I fished the swim where John had caught his big roach. About mid-morning I saw a big swirl out of the corner of my eye which was followed, shortly after, by another similar, swirl. Somehow it didn't look like a chub, so I kept close watch. Suddenly a fish (I presume it was the same one) half-swirled, half-rolled about a yard from my float, and I thought it was a roach. But I was undecided, for its size was enormous. I was just thinking what else it could have been when it rolled again, less than ten feet from me; this time I was left in no doubt. It *was* a roach, the biggest roach I have ever seen alive; certainly three pounds, possibly more. I fished on, hoping it might spot my maggots, but I never made contact. I decided there and then to flog that swim, for the sight of that tremendous roach left me shaking.

One evening I went there alone. I had planned an evening indoors writing, but shortly after tea the weather took a turn for the better – the sky darkened and it began to rain! Now if there is one fishing condition I welcome it's when the air is close and humid with either rain threatening or a fine drizzle. I mentioned this earlier in this chapter, and over the years I had called such conditions 'one of *them* nights'. (It didn't matter whether it was morning, afternoon or evening, it was always, 'night'.) Well, as I have said, it started to rain – and the air was humid. 'Stoney,' I said to myself, 'it's one of *them* nights'. Within an hour I was at the pit.

I tackled up with my usual outfit but on opening my maggot box found they had 'turned' – and maggots were the favourite bait. Still, not to worry, and a search in my haversack produced a piece of stale bread from which I mixed some very soft paste – you know, the stuff Fred J. says they 'drink instead of eating'. It certainly was soft, so soft in fact that I had difficulty in getting it on the hook. I was only fishing a rod's length out and, placing the rod in two rests, I sat back and waited.

But not for long; the float dipped slightly and stopped – then nothing. I slowly retrieved my tackle – the paste was gone. I tried again; another half-hearted bite – the paste was gone again. Fred was right – they *were* drinking it! I found another lump of bread, and with it managed to stiffen my 'drinkable' paste into an 'eatable' consistency.

The next bite took the float away and out came the first roach – all four ounces of it. Never had one so small before; still, they were about. Shortly after, I had another roachlet, then another. The next fish went to $1\frac{1}{4}$ lb., followed by one three ounces heavier, then one of 1 lb. 6 oz. By now it was too dark to see – time for a light on the float. Slowly it dipped then shot under – 2 lb. dead. I took some pictures (no picnic, at night, in rain), and packed.

The following evening, although overcast, was not one of *them*. However, flushed with success I decided to go – the writing could wait. By the time I arrived at the pit, however, the weather was better – the wind had dropped and it was raining. I almost ran to my swim.

By a strange coincidence I started off by catching three four-ounce roach. 'Aye aye,' I thought, 'it's happening again.' The drizzle persisted and it got dark; time again for the torch. As the float settled in the beam it dipped. I struck, and a heavy fish bored deep down.

Now, as I have said, a roach always swirled; no swirls and it was either a chub or tench – nuisance fish. The fish didn't swirl, and, it fought like blazes, often taking line.

'Bloody tench,' I thought, 'why doesn't it get off!'

But it didn't, and I actually tried to lose it by piling on the pressure – and, when I pile it on ... man, I really do! Only then did it come grudgingly to the net – a roach. The scales stopped at 2 lb. 2 oz. And to think I tried to lose it – whatever would Dave Steuart say!

I decided to take some pictures, only to find I had left my tripod at home. In drizzling rain and darkness under a brolly I tried to balance the camera on my haversack. I eventually managed it; then, placing my stool where I would crouch with the fish, got everything into focus. I then attached the flash – and the whole lot toppled over! I decided to abandon the idea – a simple shot on the ground would do. I fetched the roach, focused and pressed the shutter. Nothing happened – all was solid. All attempts to free it failed, and amid much colourful language I slid the roach back.

A few nights later I went there again. On the journey over the sky darkened and the atmosphere became humid. And it started to drizzle. I started off by catching a four-ounce roach – again – and my mind boggled at the thought of what was to follow. Suddenly the rain stopped, the sky cleared, and a wind blew up. Two hours later I packed – fishless.

Not one of *them* nights!

I have already mentioned the chub which are present and, of course, we caught our share. But we always regarded them as 'nuisance' fish, for once you started catching chub your chances of roach were very slim indeed.

One night I hooked a fish which I knew must be a chub because it didn't swirl, so I didn't even bother to pick up the net. But, when I saw its mouth, I had second thoughts and netted it. It was a short, thick fish and weighed $4\frac{1}{4}$ lb., and as it was such a nice-looking fish I thought I might as well have a picture. I set and focused the camera, turned on the flash then gave it to John. I picked up the chub, which, all this time, hadn't moved one inch, and held it facing the camera. As I did so it gave one almighty kick, landed in six inches of water, turned round, and shot off like a rocket!

Just before Christmas we had the first frosts, and I naturally assumed our night excursions were finished. But Fred doesn't take anything for granted and decided to carry on – frosts or no frosts. And the roach still fed madly. The following night I decided to leave the comforts of the fireside and joined him.

Another interesting fact then emerged; the roach, as usual, didn't start to feed until it had been dark for about an hour. This was both a nuisance and a help; a nuisance because (of work again) we only got two or three hours fishing in; a help, because there was no tearing hurry to get there. This meant we often tackled up in the dark – and what fun *that* caused – at least for me. Have you ever tried threading a 3-lb. line through rod rings, then tying on a No. 18 hook – sometimes in pouring rain? You haven't? Then read on, my friends, read on!

Attaching the float wasn't too bad, but with cold, wet fingers do you think I could locate the splits in the split shot? Two b.b. and a No. 7 the float takes; well the shots were 'b.s' all right – and I almost emptied the box of No. 7s before I managed it. Then came the hook – a No. 18; twice I cut the line instead of the loose end. And the rain hammered down.

I eventually got to my swim, made myself comfy, only to discover that the No. 7 shot had fallen off. I held the torch under my chin; between my knees with the light shining upwards and various other positions, all the time trying to get the line in that perishing 'split'. I finally made it – fifteen minutes, and two roach from Fred, later.

We went again the next night but this time I was really organised. Before I left home I made up a trace; now, with only a half-blood knot to tie, I should save much time – and temper. In the car headlights I tackled up, trimmed the loose end of line at the half-blood, placed the hook in the little ring above the butt and wound up the slack. But the 'slack' remained slack. I looked down; there, hanging at my feet, was the float. I looked up the rod; the rings were empty. I had cut the line.

All winter we caught roach, always at night (daytime fishing was a waste of time) and gradually our tally of big roach increased. In reflection, however, we made a big mistake; that of fishing just two swims.

Our usual swim was the one where I had seen the big roach.

By February, however, the average size of fish was dropping to around the 1¼-lb. mark, but still we pressed on. One day an angler told John that he was fishing lower down the lake at night and was catching roach to 1¾ lb. regularly. 'But,' he said, 'I can't catch a two-pounder – think I'll try somewhere else.' We discussed this, and decided to try our friend's swim.

It was much deeper than our previous one – about 8 ft. – and when we arrived roach were rolling on the surface. We began catching fish between 1½ lb. and 1¾ lb. when suddenly my float lifted to half-cock, travelled to the edge of the torch beam, then stopped. Should I strike, or not? I was undecided, for almost without question to strike with the float still showing meant a missed fish. And my float wasn't just showing; it was almost toppling over!

I chanced it, and found myself into an exceptional fish which eventually pulled the scales to 2¼ lb. John told our friend next day. His comments were unprintable!

We fished that swim until the end of the season, during which time many good roach came to net. One night an event took place which was all against the principles of night fishing; that of flashing the torch beam directly into the water.

It had been dark some time when John suddenly exclaimed: 'Here, keep quiet, take a look down by my rod rest. See it, can you? A blooming great roach!' Peering into the light of John's torch I could just make out a shape before it finally disappeared out of the beam. 'What a roach,' John continued, 'all blue it was – a real big 'un.'

The big roach returned periodically throughout the night (we assumed it was the same fish) and on three occasions it was accompanied by several others. John scattered some maggots into the area and was surprised later to see the roach upending and eating them. It was well past ten o'clock and the frost was clamping down, but I decided to try and catch one. Pulling the float down, I gently lowered my tackle into twelve inches of water with two maggots resting on the bottom. But my 8 in. float carrying two b.b.s and a No. 7 was much too hefty in the circumstances, and I wasn't surprised when a bite failed to develop. I tell you this in case you think those roach were stupid, for they were not – far from it. I can best illustrate this by relating an incident which took place in daylight. My float was shotted to within ½ in. of the tip and I was constantly bothered with bites which would not develop. Changing to one of Pete Drennan's 'Rose-Buds', I shotted it so that no more than ⅛ in. – yes, ⅛ in. – remained above the surface. I was fishing close in, of course, and the next bite just – and *only* just – pulled the float under. That roach weighed 1 lb. 10 oz.

But back to those floodlit roach. With 8 in. of float in 12 in. of water I didn't really expect a roach – or chub for that matter – to take my bait, but just after 11 o'clock a three-pound chub did just that, and was duly landed. Consider the facts. That chub had picked up my bait in 12 in. of brightly-lit water close to a rod rest less than three feet from the torch. Quite remarkable, don't you agree?

The following night we went again, and this time I took along a second rod which I intended fishing close in against John's rod rest. My float was 1¼ in. long and carried one 'dust'. Darkness came, and with it the roach which started feeding about five feet out. But with bites coming every cast I could not concentrate on a second rod, although one chub was taken on one of the few occasions I watched it. That night more big roach were seen against the torch, and I am convinced that, had I had sufficient will-power to concentrate on my spare rod, I would have caught one.

I had my final fling on the evening of March 14th. With a pile of good roach behind me that week I decided to experiment and positioned the torch so the beam shone *right into* the water. In pouring rain I caught six roach to 1¼ lb. and lost several others, despite fishing 'all wrong'.

So ended our season at the pit. Our final tally was 406 roach over the pound, with eight over two pounds. In addition we learnt a lot and a few points are, I think, worth discussing.

The most baffling thing was why the roach fed well in daytime in summer but were difficult – nay, almost impossible – to catch in daytime in winter. Secondly, why was dusk – the period 'par-excellence' for roach so unproductive? And why, in winter, was it they didn't commence feeding until well after dark – not before?

There was also this question of lights: why were they not scared by the torch shining directly into the water? This question arose on other waters with barbel, so, for a moment, I will digress. For I consider this an important question – I almost said 'break-through' – in night fishing techniques.

A friend located some barbel in a small, shallow stream and he arrived one evening in the hope of copping one. Darkness came and, as night fishing was banned, he got up to pack. Before he did so, however, he decided to see whether, in fact, the barbel were present, and shone his powerful torch into the water. The beam picked out several barbel which, to his surprise, appeared to take little notice. Calling his mate he got him to hold the torch and, with the beam still shining on the barbel, he lowered a bait in front of one. 'It was daft, really,' he told me, 'and I didn't really expect one to take, but it did.' This fish he eventually landed. This chap himself is a barbel specialist, and he, like me, had never witnessed anything quite like it before.

Other facts to emerge were the importance of using the right type of float – if one was to be consistently successful, that is; the importance of having the clutch set lightly to prevent fish from coming adrift when swirling; and the importance of consistently groundbaiting with 'cloud' and maggots. Time and time again a bite would occur immediately groundbait was introduced, often when the float hadn't moved for some time. And despite the fact that roach accepted loose maggots in midwater, to fish 'on the drop' was useless; the bait *had* to be stationary.

I always changed the maggot, too, if I thought a roach had mouthed it. Perhaps I'm over fussy – I don't know – but I have always taken the view that a big roach will not take a bait which has been touched by another of its kind – a view shared by Dick Walker.

What of the future? Will our little pit ever fish so well again?

Will the coming season (I'm writing this in May) provide us with even bigger roach – a three-pounder perhaps? Now that *is* something I would love to catch – a really big roach. What would I do with it if ever such good fortune came my way? A difficult question. But is it? – come to think of it, my bream looks pretty lonely up there, all by itself!

17. Roach and dace on Opera

Those who have fished with Dick Walker will know that he has the happy knack of being able to catch fish 'to order'. I remember a day on the Ouse when Jack Thorndike, who was then Editor of *Angling Times*, fished with us. During the afternoon Dick suddenly said, 'Ah well, I suppose I had better show these Editors that I *can* fish – think I'll catch a five-pound chub'. In less than ten minutes he was back with one – five and a half pounds.

I have, of course, seen Dick do this sort of thing many times, but on one occasion the joke was on me. Dick, like me, has a passion for Opera, but whereas I don't profess to be a singer Dick does, and often bursts into song whilst fishing, which has led to some very uncomplimentary remarks being thrown in his direction. One day, whilst in the middle of an aria, Fred J. exclaimed 'For God's sake, Dick, dry up – I can't stand it any longer!' Dick's face dropped, but suddenly brightened up again as Joe spoke. 'I think you have a nice voice, Dick,' he said. 'Trouble is, you spoil it by singing.' Roars of laughter all round.

One day Dick invited me to spend a weekend at his home. After supper on the Friday Dick played his selection of records, it being well past midnight when we retired to bed. Perhaps Dick was swotting up on his Italian, I don't know, but that is by the way. We arose early next morning, and by daybreak were on the banks of the river Beane. Dick asked me where I liked to fish, and I suggested a large 'slack' in which there was a big patch of lilies. We decided to fish alongside each other, and were soon fishing with our floats little more than six inches apart.

An hour passed – no bites. Dick knew exactly where the fish were – in a 'pocket' between some lily roots – and we watched our floats intently. Apart from recasting and inspection of baits, our floats remained stationary for over an hour.

Suddenly Dick spoke. 'Now then, Stoney,' he said, 'you thought I was pulling your leg when I told you some time ago that fish could be caught on the right song, didn't you?' I nodded. 'Right then,' he replied, 'I am going to catch some dace.' 'O.K.,' I said, 'what is the right song?' 'A bit of Giordano,' Dick said. 'Here goes.'

'*Amor to viets do non amar.*' Dick's tenor voice disturbed the peace around us. My eyes were glued to both floats and sure enough Dick's quivered. He struck, and out came a half pound dace. I couldn't believe it. He rebaited and cast again.

'*La man tua lieve che me respinge*' – another half pound dace! In the net it went, another maggot was impaled on the hook and cast amongst the lilies. '*Cerca la stretta della mia man*'; I saw the float quiver again – another big dace. '*La tua pupillae sprime t'amo sei labbro dice non t'amero*' – and out came the fourth.

For once I was speechless; after all, my float hadn't moved. I inspected the maggot; it was untouched. I recast again as close to Dick's float as possible.

But I still wasn't satisfied. 'I suppose,' I said, 'that you will now tell me that if you sing *Annie Laurie* you will catch a roach'. Walker rebaited his hook and cast. 'Like dew on the gowans lyin' is the fa' ofer fairly feet, like wind in the ...' and slowly his float dipped. It couldn't be, yet the bite was typical of a roach. Seconds later I slipped the net under a plump roach weighing a little over a pound.

I was stunned; if I hadn't seen it I would have laughed it off as a joke. Not once had my float moved, yet at no time was it more than six inches away from Dick's. The remainder of the day was spent looking at motionless floats with Walker flatly refusing to sing another note.

I've caught some fish 'to order' at different times and I've seen some funny things happen in fishing, but that one takes the biscuit!

INDEX

Annan, river, 95–9

Barbel, Kennet, 22
   Royalty, 100–4
   Thames, 13–21
Blenheim Lake, 42–8
Bream, gravel-pit, 111–12
   Thames, 64–73

Catfish, 31–2
Chub, Annan, 95–9
   Five-pound, 58–63
   Upper Ouse, 49–57

Eels, Conger, 36–7

Freeze-up, 1963, 105–9

Gravel-pit, 110–22

Kennet river, 22–9

Monkfish, 41

Mullet, creek, 79–80

Ouse, Upper, 49–57
Oxford Specimen Group, 18, 20, 46

Perch, 30–1, 52–3
Pike, 42–8, 108–9
Pollack, 35

Quiver-tip, 55–7

Roach, 53–7, 111–24
Royalty fishery, 100–4

Sea fishing, 34–41, 79–80
Sharks, 34–5
Snowberry Lake, 30–3

Television, fishing for, 81–6
Tench, 87–94
Tope, 38–40
Trout, on fly, 74–8